THE POCKET

IDIOT'S GUIDE™ TO

Investing in Bonds

by Ken Little

ALPHA

A member of Penguin Group (USA) Inc.

To my wife, best friend, and cabinmate, Cyndy, who tolerates my long absences from family responsibilities while I write.

ALPHA BOOKS

Published by the Penguin Group

Penguin Group (USA) Inc., 375 Hudson Street, New York, New York 10014, USA

Penguin Group (Canada), 90 Eglinton Avenue East, Suite 700, Toronto, Ontario M4P 2Y3, Canada (a division of Pearson Penguin Canada Inc.)

Penguin Books Ltd, 80 Strand, London WC2R 0RL, England

Penguin Ireland, 25 St. Stephen's Green, Dublin 2, Ireland (a division of Penguin Books Ltd.)

Penguin Group (Australia), 250 Camberwell Road, Camberwell, Victoria 3124, Australia (a division of Pearson Australia Group Pty. Ltd.)

Penguin Books India Pvt. Ltd., 11 Community Centre, Panchsheel Park, New Delhi—110 017, India

Penguin Group (NZ), 67 Apollo Drive, Rosedale, North Shore, Auckland 1311, New Zealand (a division of Pearson New Zealand Ltd.)

Penguin Books (South Africa) (Pty.) Ltd, 24 Sturdee Avenue, Rosebank, Johannesburg 2196, South Africa

Penguin Books Ltd., Registered Offices: 80 Strand, London WC2R 0RL, England

International Standard Book Number: 978-1-59257-629-6
Library of Congress Catalog Card Number: 2007922822

09 08 07   8 7 6 5 4 3 2 1

Interpretation of the printing code: The rightmost number of the first series of numbers is the year of the book's printing; the rightmost number of the second series of numbers is the number of the book's printing. For example, a printing code of 07-1 shows that the first printing occurred in 2007.

Printed in the United States of America

Note: This publication contains the opinions and ideas of its author. It is intended to provide helpful and informative material on the subject matter covered. It is sold with the understanding that the author and publisher are not engaged in rendering professional services in the book. If the reader requires personal assistance or advice, a competent professional should be consulted.

The author and publisher specifically disclaim any responsibility for any liability, loss, or risk, personal or otherwise, which is incurred as a consequence, directly or indirectly, of the use and application of any of the contents of this book.

Most Alpha books are available at special quantity discounts for bulk purchases for sales promotions, premiums, fund-raising, or educational use. Special books, or book excerpts, can also be created to fit specific needs.

For details, write: Special Markets, Alpha Books, 375 Hudson Street, New York, NY 10014.

Contents

Introduction

If you are like many investors, you know that bonds are supposed to be part of a balanced portfolio. You also know you're supposed to eat five to eight servings of vegetables and fruits every day. This simply proves that *knowing* you should do something and actually *doing it* are two different things.

I can't help you with your diet, but I can get you started toward understanding the important role bonds play in your portfolio. That first step comes with a better understanding of what bonds are, the different types of bonds, and how you can use that knowledge to improve your investing.

We'll start off with an overview of how bonds differ from shares of stock and discuss why you should have them in your portfolio. Not all bonds are the same, so I'll go over the three different types.

Many investors think "bonds" and "safety" are synonyms. While that may be true about some bonds (U.S. Treasury issues), it is not true of every bond issue. Some bonds carry a high degree of risk, and depending on your intended use, almost all bonds have more risk than you might imagine. Sound investing begins with understanding risk.

The bond market is different from the stock market in many ways. How it operates and how bonds are bought and sold add to your understanding of how you can use bonds to diversify your portfolio. I spend a full chapter on each type of bond: U.S. Treasury, municipal, and corporate, so you can appreciate the differences and similarities.

The math behind bond valuation can be confusing. Terms that sound very much alike have different meanings. It is important for investors to understand how interest rate changes in particular affect the value of bonds.

Some investors find bond mutual funds the answer to their bond-investing dilemma; however, that opens up another can of worms—which fund or funds? Bond mutual funds come in many different configurations, and I'll help you sift through the assortment for those that work best.

Finally, I'll put it together with suggestions about constructing a bond portfolio. You won't find a get-rich-quick scheme or "bond secrets," but sensible information to help you add bonds to your portfolio in a manner that benefits you.

When you finish this book, you will have the basic information you need to make better decisions about bonds and investing.

Extras

Throughout this book you will find sidebars that add bits of information to help you understand and use bonds more effectively. Each one has its own visual clue.

def•i•ni•tion

These are definitions of industry terms that will help you through the jargon.

Red Flag

These are warnings about the different aspects of investing in bonds that can be potential pitfalls.

Bond Tip

These are bits of advice on how to get the most out of your bond investment or how to use a tool more effectively.

Market Place

These are interesting facts and insights about the bond investment industry.

Acknowledgments

Thanks, once again, to Paul Dinas of Alpha Books for the opportunity to work with this fine publishing house.

I also want to thank my wife, Cyndy, for her support during the long hours needed to complete my book projects. She has never complained and has shouldered more than her share of caring for our family while I worked on deadlines.

Her careful day-to-day management of family resources helps me remember that keeping expenses low is a major component of success in personal finance and investing.

Special Thanks to the Technical Reviewer

The Pocket Idiot's Guide to Investing in Bonds was reviewed by an expert who double-checked the accuracy of what you'll learn here, to help us ensure that this book gives you everything you need to know about investing in bonds. Special thanks are extended to Ken Kaplan.

Trademarks

Why Bonds?

In This Chapter

- All about bonds
- Special bond terms
- Role of bonds in investing
- Types of bonds

"Stocks and bonds." You hear the two words used together so often, you might think they were two sides of the same coin. They both are involved in investing and you probably should have both in your portfolio; however, that's where much of the similarity ends.

Bonds often march to a different economic drummer and that's one reason to add them to your portfolio. Most bonds also pay a steady stream of current income, which makes them a choice selection for people who are looking for that feature in an investment.

Bonds even offer the potential for capital gain, through trading them much like other investors trade stocks.

Investing in bonds does have its challenges and, depending on the type of bond you select, even significant risk, as we'll see in later chapters.

Introduction to Bonds

A bond represents a debt owed by the issuing organization. Governmental entities and corporations issue or sell bonds to raise money for a variety of reasons. Investors who buy the bonds, the bondholders, are the lenders.

Bonds as Legal Debts

Bondholders are lenders to corporations and government agencies. Most bonds require the corporation or governmental agency to pay interest at a prescribed rate for a defined period. Think of bonds as a loan agreement between you (the bondholder) and the corporation or governmental entity (the issuer). Like any loan, there is a repayment schedule that calls for payments on certain dates until the loan is paid off.

A loan you take out (car loan, for example), usually requires you to pay back some principal and interest with each payment. Most bonds only pay interest and then repay the principal in a lump sum at the end.

Common Features of Most Bonds

When bonds are issued, the terms are spelled out and remain fixed for the life of the bond. Specifically, the bond will state the face value, the interest rate it pays, how often interest payments are made, its maturity date, and any special features or provisions. A document called the *indenture agreement* gives the complete details of each bond. It is published just before the bond is issued.

def•i•ni•tion

> The **indenture agreement** is a binding legal document between the organization issuing the bonds and the bondholder. It details the maturity, interest payments, collateral, and other important information.

You can know all the details of each new bond issue before you make a decision to buy. No surprises.

Bonds Are Different Than Stocks

Bonds are a legal debt that must be repaid. Bondholders are repaid before many other debts in the event of a bankruptcy and have a claim on assets for repayment ahead of stockholders.

As a holder of stock, you are a part owner of the company. You are entitled to share in the profits and participate in key decisions such as electing the board of directors. If the company does very well, you participate in that success and can potentially earn large returns (ask early investors in Microsoft how it's worked for them). Other companies pay steady and rising dividends quarter after quarter, year after year, and the stock usually rises in price also.

On the other hand, with that potential reward comes the possibility that your investment will fly like a lead balloon. Remember all the super-stocks of the dot.com bull market that, in fact, nobody can remember because they have disappeared. You can also lose all of your investment—but no more that that—by investing in stocks.

Bonds don't offer the "upside" potential of stocks. They may gain in market price under the right conditions; however, it is very unlikely bonds will ever offer the type of gains you potentially can earn from stocks.

 Red Flag

Anywhere there is a large amount of money (as there exists in the bond market), you will find sophisticated trading strategies that attempt to beat the market. Be careful of any trading strategy or product you don't fully understand. Most of these apparently sophisticated strategies are successful in generating commissions for sales people and not much else.

On the other hand, if you have chosen your bond investments with care, you will not lose your principal if you hold the bond until maturity or trade it for a profit. Most bonds pay a steady income that you can count on for as long as you own the bond or until maturity.

Stocks and Bonds as Marketable Securities

Both stocks and bonds are bought and sold on the open market. This means you can buy and sell bonds before their maturity, which many people do. Although there are some similarities in the way the mechanics work, there are major differences also. As we dig deeper into the subject, you'll see how these differences create both challenges and opportunities.

Basic Bond Terms

Investing in bonds, like investing in stocks, has special terms that identify the major parts and movements of bonds and bond transactions. Many of these terms will be familiar if you are a stock or mutual fund investor; however, a few take on a slightly different meaning when referring to bonds.

Principal, Face Value

You may hear principal or face value refer to the amount of the bond's principal amount. This is the usual amount you will receive when the bond matures. For example, a $1,000, 10-year Treasury note will pay the owner $1,000 when the bond matures in 10 years. For most bonds, the principal and face value are the original amount of the bond; however, there are some bonds you buy for less than the face value. For example, zero-coupon bonds are sold at a deep discount to face value, but you receive the full face value at maturity. The difference is the interest the bond earns. Zero-coupon bonds are explained in detail in Chapter 10.

Market Value, Par Value, Premium, and Discount

Since bonds can be bought and sold before their maturity on the *secondary market*, they also have a market value. A bond's market value is determined by its coupon rate (the interest rate paid by the bond), the current market interest rate, and time to maturity, along with other factors such as creditworthiness. If you buy or sell a bond before maturity, it will be at its market value, not face value. Depending on the factors just cited, the market value may be higher or lower than the face value.

def•i•ni•tion

> The **secondary market** is the open market between individuals or through an exchange where previously issued bonds are bought and sold. A bond can be bought and sold many times before its maturity.

If the market value is the same as the principal, or face value, the bond is trading at par. If the bond is trading at a market price higher than face value, it is trading at a premium and, you guessed it, the bond is trading at a discount if the market price is less than the face value.

Issuer

New bonds are issued by corporations, the U.S. Treasury, and other governmental entities. It is important to know the issuer because part of a bond's value is determined by the credit quality of the issuer. If the organization issuing the bonds is very creditworthy, the bonds will be issued with a lower interest rate (for the lower risk of default). If the issuer has bad credit, it will have to offer higher interest rates to attract investors and compensate them for the additional risks.

Coupon Rate

Coupon rate or coupon is the interest rate applied to the principal to give you the annual interest payment for the bond. For example, a $1,000 bond with a coupon rate of 6 percent will pay an annual interest payment of $60. Most interest payments are made twice a year, but not always. In this example, you would receive two payments of $30.

You will also hear the coupon expressed as the annual interest payment. For example, you might hear a bond referred to as having a $60 coupon. This is historically more accurate, since years ago bonds where issued with coupons, which investors had to clip and mail in to receive their payment—hence the term "coupon clippers" as a reference to bondholders.

Either way the coupon is expressed, you know what the bond will pay in annual interest payments. For most bonds, the coupon or coupon rate remains constant for the life of the bond.

Maturity

Bonds have a beginning and an end. When the bond is issued there is an end date called the maturity. On this date, bondholders get the principal paid to them. As noted, bonds trade like stocks, between investors. However, it does not matter what the market price of the bond is at maturity. The person who owns the bond will be paid the face value of the bond at maturity. For example, a bondholder may have a $1,000, 5-year bond that has a market value of $1,200. However, when it matures the owner will receive $1,000, plus he will have received $60 per year in interest payments for a total of $1,300.

Market Place

Most bonds have maturities under 30 years, but not all. Walt Disney, among others, has issued bonds with maturities of 100 years. In England, they issue an instrument similar to a bond called a perpetual bond that has no maturity—it pays forever.

Call Provision

The call provision comes into play when the issuer decides it can refinance its debt at a lower interest rate than the bonds. This is bad news for the bondholder, although you don't "lose" money, per se—you are repaid the face value in full. What you do lose are those interest payments you were counting on for your retirement or some other financial goal.

You get your principal back, but now must reinvest the money at an often lower interest rate (rates have usually fallen, that's why the issuer has called the bonds) if you buy a new bond. Your loss is the difference in what you earned with the original bond and what is available now and at what cost.

Many municipal and corporate bonds contain this type of little bombshell for unsuspecting investors. Watch for these types of provisions.

Yield or Yield-to-Maturity

When you hear news commentators talk about a bond's yield, they usually mean the "yield-to-maturity." This is a calculation that gives a return that considers the interest rate, current (or market) price, and time to maturity. There are several other "yield" measurements that we'll discuss in later chapters.

Valuing bonds can be a little confusing, so we spend a whole chapter talking about the subject (Chapter 8).

Why Investors Own Bonds

There are two reasons investors own bonds: for their negative correlation to stocks and for their income. Bonds respond to many economic and market stimuli differently than stocks, while providing a steady cash flow and the relative certainty of getting your principal back when the bond matures.

Respond to Different Economic Forces

Bonds are said to have a negative correlation to stocks, which means as stocks move one direction, bonds tend to move the opposite direction. This negative correlation is one way investors diversify their holdings so not all of their portfolio is moving in the same direction.

Interest rates and inflation, often the evil siblings of economic undoing, drive the bond market crazy. There is no doubt that both factors also affect stocks, but not necessarily in the same way or to the same degree.

News of rising inflation can send shivers through the stock market because that usually means the Federal Reserve Board will raise interest rates, which increases the cost of doing business and slows the economy. However, stocks are a relatively good hedge against inflation, because over time, companies can raise prices in response to inflation.

Bonds, on the other hand, are stuck. For the most part, a bond's interest rate and maturity are fixed. If interest rates and/or inflation rise, existing bonds fall in value because newer debt issues will be at higher interest rates.

When the economy is slowing and interest rates are dropping, bonds may perform better than stocks because of their steady income streams and locked-in interest rates. In down economies, companies' earnings are flat and stocks may suffer, but bonds continue paying their steady income.

Historic Alternative to Stocks

Bonds are typically bought for their income and as a balance or buffer to the volatility of the stocks in a portfolio. The main feature of most bonds is the income stream (usually two interest payments per year, but not always). This income makes bonds a viable alternative to other income-producing products such as bank certificates of deposit, preferred stocks, and so on.

As a buffer to stocks, the bond's income stream remains constant regardless of turmoil in the market. Events that may cause stock prices to jump all over the charts have no effect on the income stream generated by your bond. While the return you can get from most bonds will never approach the potential gains of a strong stock, that semi-annual interest payment will look very attractive when your high-flying stock is in the dumps.

Three Strategies for Bonds

Investors have three broad ways to use bonds: hold them to maturity; buy and sell them for profit; or invest in bonds using mutual funds or exchange-traded funds.

What Do You Want to Accomplish with Bonds?

Your investment in bonds should fit a specific financial purpose or goal. You can use bonds to meet several goals and different strategies for each. Before you can decide what role bonds play in your portfolio, it might be helpful to look at three basic ways you can employ bonds in your strategy. We'll discuss all three of these strategies in more detail throughout the book, but an overview might be helpful as an introduction.

> **Bond Tip**
>
> Approach bond investing with a goal in mind; this way you can match the characteristics of the bond with your financial goal. The goal should include expected return, risk, and time frame.

You Can Hold Them

Many investors buy bonds and hold them to their maturity. This is particularly true of U.S. Treasury bonds and notes, since you can buy them directly without paying a commission to a broker.

Investors wanting current income and a higher yield
and willing to take more risk might look at a highly
rated corporate bond. High-income investors may
be interested in the tax-free income from municipal
bonds.

When you buy a bond with the intention to hold it
until maturity, your main concerns are:

- Will the bond be called? Many corporate
  and municipal bonds have call provisions
  that allow the issuers to redeem the bonds
  before maturity if interest rates fall. Investors receive their investment back, but lose
  the opportunity to earn a higher interest
  rate because they must reinvest the bond
  proceeds at now lower rates.

- Will the issuer default? Investors can protect
  themselves from default by only purchasing
  bonds with high ratings by the independent
  agencies that monitor bond issuers' creditworthiness.

If you have no plan to sell the bond before maturity,
the market price of your bond is of no real concern
to you, since it is the face value that will be paid to
you at maturity.

You Can Buy and Sell Bonds for Profit

Some investors find profit in trading bonds on
the secondary market. They buy and sell bonds
like other investors trade stocks. An investor may
hold a bond for several years, enjoying the income

stream and then selling for a profit, perhaps antici-
pating interest rate changes (and perhaps changes
in creditworthiness) may discount the bond in the
near future.

You can begin as a "buy and hold" investor with
bonds and change your mind several years out for
any number of reasons. If you buy Treasury-issued
bonds, you shouldn't have trouble finding a market
for your bond (but not necessarily the price you
want).

If you buy municipal or corporate bonds, it's a little
trickier as we'll explore in later chapters. There is
not a ready market for every bond, so finding the
price you want may be difficult. If you plan to sell
your bond before maturity, make sure it is one that
is actively traded so there will be a market for it
when the time comes to sell.

Using Mutual Funds and Exchange-Traded Funds

Many investors find bonds complicated and confusing, so they turn to professionally managed funds
to handle the bonds side of their portfolio. A bond
mutual fund is a professionally managed portfolio
of bonds with stated investment objectives. Investors rely on professionals to make buy and sell
decisions. Exchange-traded funds (ETFs) are very
similar to bond mutual funds except they track an
index of bonds and are traded like stock on the open
market. Using one of these types of funds is often
an excellent strategy; however, investing in a bond

fund is not the same as investing in an individual bond. There are some benefits and drawbacks that you should consider before picking this route. We'll explore this more later in the book, including some of the risks, which are covered in Chapter 3.

> **Market Place**
>
> Bond funds and exchange-traded funds offer an easy way to add bonds to your portfolio; however, they may not accomplish what you want if you are a "buy and hold" investor with a specific goal in mind. Bond funds and ETFs are not predictable like the face value and income stream of an individual bond.

Different Types of Bonds

Bonds come in a variety of types and from different issuers, which gives investors a wide range of investment options. Investors should be able to find a bond type that matches their financial goals.

Bonds Come from a Variety of Issuers

Bonds are issued as debt obligations by the U.S. government, state and local governments, and corporations. Because of the diversity of issuers, it is important to distinguish between the types of bonds. While some basic characteristics extend across all types of bonds, individual features of the different issuers give bonds different opportunities and challenges for investors. It is unwise to think "a bond is a bond is a bond," because that simply isn't the case, as you will see in this overview and in a more detailed look at each bond type in later chapters.

U.S. Government Issues

The U.S. Treasury is the largest single issuer of bonds in the United States and maybe the world. It issues a variety of bonds that finance the workings (mainly the debt) of the U.S. government.

Your Safest Investment

U.S. Treasury issues are considered the safest investment you can make, because there is zero chance for default. The full faith and credit of the United States government backs the issues, and that's as good as it gets. The securities are so safe investors from all over the world buy them as a secure place to hold their assets.

Treasury issues come in a variety of maturities and with different features. Regardless of the differences, they all carry the same protection.

Treasury Bills

Treasury bills are the shortest maturing issues offered by the Treasury. T-bills, as they are known, mature in one, three, or six months. They are unique among Treasury issues in that you buy them at a discount to face value and the difference is the interest you earn. For example, say a six-month T-bill with a face value of $1,000 is priced at $970 and in six months get back $1,000. Your return on this six-month T-bill is 3.09 percent ($30 ÷ $970).

Treasury Notes

These are intermediate term bonds, maturing in two to ten years. Treasury notes pay interest semi-annually. They are sold usually once a month by the Treasury with minimum denominations of $1,000.

Market Place

The 10-year Treasury note has become the long-term benchmark for many financial situations. The 30-year Treasury bond used to fill that role, but it was discontinued for a number of years and has only been reissued since 2006.

Treasury Bonds

These bonds have maturities extending beyond 10 years, with some going to 30 years. Some of the longer-term bonds have a call provision.

Savings Bonds

If you haven't taken a look recently, the EE and I savings bonds have had a makeover. They offer some attractive features that make them worthy of consideration as legitimate investments and not just gifts for children. Old savings bonds used to sit in safe deposit boxes and in shoe boxes collecting interest and dust. There was not much more you could do with them. Chapter 5 has details on the evolution of savings bonds.

Treasury Inflation-Protected Securities

These bonds are fairly new on the scene, but have attracted a lot of attention. They offer a provision that lets the principal adjust to the rate of inflation, which is one of the big risks for bondholders. Treasury Inflation-Protected bonds adjust the interest rate paid based on the inflation rate, which overcomes a big drawback for regular bonds.

Agency Securities

Several agencies within the federal government issue bonds that offer rates slightly above Treasury issues. Although they are not completely backed by the full faith and credit of the U.S. government, they are thought to be very secure. Many of the bonds are related to housing agencies and are mortgage pass-throughs and similar bonds. Mortgage pass-through bonds are tied to residential mortgages and investors receive some principal and interest with each payment.

Buying Treasury Issues

Except for agency securities, which you buy through a broker, you can buy Treasury issues directly from the government if you wish and avoid paying any commission. It is a simple transaction you can do over the phone or online via the U.S. Treasury website. Chapter 5 explains the process in detail.

Municipal Bonds

State and local governments issue bonds to pay for a variety of projects such as building roads, bridges, and other infrastructure components. Income from municipal bonds is generally exempt from federal income tax and generally local taxes for investors who live in the state where the bonds are issued.

Financing Local Projects

"Municipal bond" is a catch-all phrase that covers bonds issued by state governments and agencies, counties and their agencies, and cities and their agencies. In short, the term municipal bond generally refers to an issue by a governmental body or related entity within the geographic boundaries of a single state.

There is usually one main reason investors consider "munis," as they are called, and that's the exemption from federal income tax on the interest paid. This makes municipal bonds very attractive to investors in high tax brackets and can even work for those investors without millions.

If you buy a municipal bond within the boundaries of your own state, the interest may be exempt from state and local income tax (if collected) also. You can find mutual funds that offer state-specific bond funds that invest in these "double or triple tax-free" bonds. A stockbroker that specializes in bonds can help you find these issues.

Types of Municipal Bonds

There are generally two types of municipal bonds, although you will find considerable creativity in the market with issuers. The bulk of the issues, however, will be either:

- General obligation bonds—These bonds are backed by the maximum legal taxing authority of the government unit issuing the bonds. This means the voters have usually agreed to a portion of the tax revenue going to repay the debt.

- Revenue bonds—These bonds are repaid out of income generated by the project financed by the bonds. An example of a revenue bond would be an issue used to build a toll road, with revenue from collected tolls earmarked to repay the bonds. Revenue bonds are considered slightly more risky than general obligation bonds, so you should get a higher coupon rate.

Bond Tip

Municipal bonds are often sold in large denominations—$5,000 per bond and a five-bond trading unit. Municipal bonds are usually bought for the tax advantages, so many investors find mutual funds a better option than individual bonds.

Corporate Bonds

Companies use bonds to finance many different projects when long-term financing is needed. Corporate bonds can be on the high end of the risk scale, but pay higher returns.

Corporate Bonds and Higher Returns

Investors wanting higher returns and willing to step out with some risk look to corporate bonds. Companies issue bonds to finance a variety of projects, including new facilities and equipment or acquisitions. Issuing bonds is often cheaper than borrowing money from a bank or a long-term lender. Corporations may not want to issue new stock to raise the needed capital.

Since corporations have neither the ability to collect taxes nor the right to print money, their bonds carry the greatest overall degree of risk. Corporations are legally obligated to pay bondholders. In the event of a default, bondholders have first call on the assets of a company, meaning the assets can be seized and sold to pay off the bondholders. However, if you stick to highly rated issues, the risk of default is low. There is more about bond ratings in Chapter 3.

Two main features to consider in corporate bonds:

- Convertible bonds—These bonds, which can be very attractive in the right situation, give the bondholder the right to convert the bond into shares of common stock under predetermined conditions. Usually, convertible bonds set a target stock price above the current price when the bonds are issued. If the stock hits the target price, the bondholder can convert the bond to shares of stock. Investors buy convertible bonds so they can earn interest on the bonds and convert to shares of stock if the price rises. If the price of the stock doesn't rise, the investor still has the income from the bond.

- Call provision—Most corporate bonds have a call provision that gives the company the right to call or redeem the bond for its full face value on or after a certain date. A corporation can call a bond issue in if interest rates have fallen and it can refinance its debt at a lower interest rate.

Corporate bonds are covered in detail in Chapter 6.

The Least You Need to Know

- Bonds represent a debt obligation and the bondholder is the lender.
- The U.S. Treasury and federal agencies along with other governmental entities and corporations issue bonds to finance a variety of projects and needs.
- The face value of a bond is the amount the bondholder receives when the bond matures.
- The coupon or coupon rate represents the annual payment to the bondholder.

Chapter 2

How the Bond Market Works

In This Chapter

- Overview of bond markets
- Active versus passive management
- Market's best estimate of the value
- Difficulties with picking bonds
- Expenses and returns
- Where bonds are sold

The bond market may seem like a strange place to newcomers and they would be correct. Although many of the same forces that operate in the stock market are present in the bond market, it is still a different place.

The market described in this chapter is where bonds are bought and sold. We'll discuss the actual mechanics of how you buy and sell bonds in Chapter 4. This chapter focuses on the bigger picture, but still gives you some very concrete advice—in fact, the most important piece of investing advice you'll find in this book is in this chapter. Parts of this investing advice are also repeated in later chapters because it's so important, but you read it here first.

A Brief Overview of How Markets Work

The secondary market where bonds are traded operates by certain economic principles. Some view the market as a place where hard work and intelligence will win, while others say the market is too efficient to allow anyone to consistently know more than the market does.

Competing Wisdom in the Market

Don't worry, this isn't going to be a lot of academic double-talk. It is going to introduce two visions of how the bond market works and why you should care. Having a basic understanding of what is happening could save you many dollars and some frustration. One vision suggests that smart people, working hard, can beat the market with their bond picks. The second vision says the market is highly efficient and active management will not produce consistently superior results and may do more harm than good by incurring extra trading costs.

Incidentally, as a bonus, much of this discussion applies to investing in stocks as well.

Market Place

Stock pickers and bond pickers may disagree with some of this chapter and point to examples of people (perhaps themselves) who have beaten the market many times. Of all the people who invest, only a very small percentage of active traders beat the market with any consistency. More importantly, there is no guarantee an investment strategy that works today will produce the same results in a future market under different circumstances.

What Salespeople Will Tell You

This is not a slam at bond (or stock) brokers. They have a job to do and perform a valuable service. If you are going to buy individual corporate or municipal bonds, you will need a good broker who specializes in bonds. However, you must be careful about brokers who claim a special talent or system for consistently doing better than the overall market. As you'll see, this is not a skill you can count on with any consistency.

Before we dive into the two visions of how the bond market works, we need to look at the two methods of managing your investments: active management versus passive management.

Methods for Managing Your Investments

The two types of investment management are active and passive, and they reflect the role of the investor or mutual fund manager in directing the investments. In addition, a major distinction between the two styles is the expense involved in active management (research, trading costs, and so on) versus the relatively low cost of passive management, which features much less activity.

Active Management

In most cases, active management refers to the style employed by many mutual fund managers. An actively managed mutual fund is one that will feature frequent trades as the manager seeks to profit from situations that he spots in the market. Actively managed bond funds will move into and out of positions as market conditions change, trading frequently in an attempt to strengthen their position.

Individual investors can also actively manage their money in much the same manner by trading frequently to take advantage of potential market bargains. The problem for individual investors in the bond market is that trading corporate and municipal bonds requires a broker, and paying commissions can quickly eat into any profits. In addition, individuals usually pay a higher price for bonds than money managers because of smaller purchases.

> **Bond Tip**
>
> You can tell an actively managed bond mutual fund by the load factor or sales charge, which is applied to your account either on the front end or back end. This fee drags down your profits and increases your losses.

Passive Management

Passive management is best evidenced by mutual funds built around a market index. In the world of stock investing, the most popular index mutual fund is the S&P 500 Index fund offered by numerous investment companies. In the bond world, the Vanguard Total Bond Market Fund is a popular bond index fund.

Index funds mimic the index by holding all or a substantial portion of the assets in the index. They are passive investments because the fund manager doesn't buy or sell bonds in the funds unless the composition of the index changes, which is not often. The advantage of this type of investing is there are no research costs to pay for and very little in the way of transaction costs to cover. With lower costs, index fund and passive investing put more of your investment dollars to work than active investing, which must cover the cost of research and its trading costs.

Individuals who buy bonds and hold them until maturity are practicing a form of passive investing.

If you buy a newly issued corporate or municipal bond, the commission is paid by the issuer. If you choose a U.S. Treasury issue, you can buy directly from the Treasury and avoid commissions altogether. If you use a broker to buy a previously issued bond, you only pay one commission (to buy the bond).

Management Style and Market Wisdom

Whether you use active or passive management of your bond assets has a direct bearing on your potential return. The two visions of how the market works take different approaches to using active or passive management.

Efficient Market Theory

The efficient market theory (EMT) says that securities priced in the market are the best estimates of their real value because of the efficient pricing mechanism of the market.

The EMT is fairly simple to grasp. It says that the markets are very efficient at disseminating news and information about a bond (or stock), so the price reflects the market's best estimate of the value. If some new information is revealed or conditions change, the price is quickly updated by the market.

The EMT is not a new idea. It has been the subject of study for over half a century, and the conclusions are all much the same: active management doesn't add much in the way of value.

What this says in practice is that you can't know more than any other investor, so identifying a winning security that is unknown to the rest of the market is unlikely. The conclusion is that active management adds little to the process and is more likely to hurt performance because of the expenses involved.

Exceptions to the Rule

The EMT doesn't say it is impossible for some investors to do better than the market—that clearly happens. What the EMT does say is that you can't know which investors are going to "beat the market" in advance, because their past performance is not a reliable indicator of future success. The caveat you see on all financial products, "Past performance does not indicate future success," is not just an idle regulatory warning. It is empirical evidence that has been proven time and again. Just because an investor or fund manager has had some good success does not mean this year will be good also. Conventional wisdom would say follow the winner; EMT says there is no evidence after 50-plus years of research that past performance is an indicator of future success.

The other exception that you must consider is that the market could be wrong. This was certainly the case in the late 1990s stock market when it went crazy over Internet and technology-based stocks. The exuberance in the market got out of hand and drove prices of any stock connected with the Internet through the roof. A prudent investor would have seen this imbalance in the market and positioned her portfolio to take advantage of the inevitable bust.

The market can be too optimistic or pessimistic about interest rates, which can drive up or down bond prices. If an investor is wise enough to pick up on this and willing to risk the chance that he may be wrong and not the market, there would be profits in preparing for the market to correct itself.

> **Red Flag**
>
> No offense, but you are probably not the smartest bond investor in the market. There is a grave risk when you begin to believe you see opportunities that no one else can see. This is the time for a reality check. Maybe you have spotted an opportunity, but maybe you have misread the situation. Time to double-check your idea—bounce it off a trusted advisor who is knowledgeable and see if they come to the same conclusion. Maybe you *are* the smartest bond investor in the market.

The Prudent Vision of the Market

The EMT suggests to investors that outpicking (outguessing, really) the market is a losing strategy in the long run. If we could invest on past returns, we would all be rich, but that's not the way the market works. We must invest on the promise of future returns and no one can promise future success based on past performance. Sifting through mutual funds looking for the ones with the best performance over the past three to five years will not necessarily turn up any candidates that will "beat the market" next year.

Why Actively Managing Bonds Is Difficult

The EMT says it is not likely that a manager can consistently pick winners over a long period—whether it's bonds or stocks—and bonds are harder.

Why Bonds Are More Difficult to Pick

Bonds present a greater challenge to investors because of their fixed components. When an investor sets out to find a winning stock, there are all sorts of variables to consider, including the quality of management as well as pure economic or market indicators. Some of the valuation of a company is subjective, such as gauging the ability of a new manager to turn the company around, for example. An astute investor may find success in analyzing companies on many levels, not just the numbers alone.

It is different for bonds. Two highly rated bonds of the same maturity will yield about the same return. Picking one bond over the other will not likely result in any change in performance. A manager can't add much to that decision.

The big mover of bond prices is interest rates. Here, an active manager would need to call the turn when interest rates were going to change direction or stop moving temporarily. Interest rate changes are driven by changes in the economy, so an active manager who could see far enough out to predict the changes in the economy that would influence interest rates could add great value.

The problem is no one, not even economists, can look very far into the future and predict the economy. Despite what you might read in the financial press, economic forecasts that look much beyond six months are not any better than guessing. Even when a group of economists is polled and a consensus estimate is generated, the results are the same: a guess.

Another factor that affects individual bonds is a change in creditworthiness. Bond-rating companies review their scores on a regular basis and if an issuer has a change of circumstances, the rating company may downgrade an existing bond issue. This will cause the market value of the bond issue to drop.

> **Bond Tip**
>
> If you stick with highly rated bonds or U.S. Treasury issues and match maturities to your financial goals, the individual bond you pick is less important than you might think. There are other issues to consider, such as liquidity, which is discussed in Chapters 3 and 4.

Liquidity an Issue

Unlike most stocks, bonds may not have the ready market for a seller who needs to unload a losing position. If you are going to trade bonds, you must stick with issues that are well known and are widely held so the chances of finding a buyer when you are ready to sell are good.

Even if you are a buy-and-hold investor, circumstances change and you may need to sell your bond before maturity. If the bond you own is paying more than current interest rates, it might not be hard to sell. However, if it is paying the market interest rate and doesn't have any extra attractive features, you may find it is difficult to sell. If your bond is paying below-market interest rates, you will not sell it for face value, meaning you will have to discount the bond, perhaps substantially, to sell it.

What's a Bond Investor to Do?

Bond investors aren't completely at the mercy of the economy and interest rates. As we'll see in Chapter 4, there are strategies for protecting yourself and taking advantage of changing interest rates.

The bond market, however, remains a different place than the stock market, although some of the same basic principles apply as keys to investing success. The first key to investing success, whether in the stock market or bond market, is to keep your expenses as low as possible.

Improving Your Chances for a Good Return

The best way to improve your chance of investment success is directly tied to the expenses involved in making the investment. The lower the expenses, the better chance the investment will provide the hoped-for returns.

Expenses Drag on Profits

The reason actively managed investing has such a difficult time providing superior returns is the expense involved. For bond fund managers, there is the cost of research (staff salaries, and so on), the expense of buying and selling bonds (trading costs), and the administration of the fund, including commissions for selling the fund's shares. In addition, short-term buying and selling of bonds creates tax liabilities that further reduce the return to fund shareholders.

All of these expenses must be covered by profits from investing before any profit goes to the bond fund investors. Some bond funds are more efficient at actively managing than others and, over time, these differences in expenses will usually show in performance. However, this drag on fund profits is usually hard to overcome and may make it difficult to consistently earn a high return for investors.

Likewise, individual investors often incur heavy trading costs if they use a broker for their bond trades. These commissions eat into any profit and make earning acceptable profits difficult.

> **Bond Tip**
>
> Your best investment advice after sticking with highly rated bonds is to keep your investment expenses as low as possible—the lower your investment costs, the greater your chances of a higher return on your investment.

Keep Expenses Low for a Better Return

If you keep your investing expenses low, will you be successful in bond investing? Not necessarily, but you will improve your returns on good investments.

Passive bond index funds or low-expense actively managed funds give you the best chance for good returns over time. Low expenses are a key indicator that the fund has a good chance for positive returns, just as high expenses almost always mean a fund has less chance for consistently doing better than the market.

For investors who want to own individual bonds, keeping investing expense low is a challenge. You can stick with U.S. Treasury issues, which you can buy direct and skip the broker's commission. However, if you want corporate or municipal bonds, you'll need a good broker. Brokers often bury their commission in the price of the bond, so ask for full disclosure when buying from a broker and shop around for the best deal on commissions. There is more information on finding a bond broker in Chapter 4.

Buy and Hold or Trade

Trading bonds or bond mutual funds is one strategy to make money with bonds. The other strategy is to buy and hold individual bonds until they mature or buy a bond index fund or low-cost managed fund and hold it for a long period.

Consider Your Strategy

The usual bond investor who buys and holds a bond until its maturity is often looking for the current income generated by the semiannual interest checks she receives. Investors can use bonds to generate current income to fund retirement or some other financial goal. For example, if you knew you needed $10,000 in three years for a college tuition payment, you could buy a bond with a three-year maturity and enjoy the income from the bond in the three years before the bond matured and was required for other expenses. You could accomplish the same goal with a bank CD, so you would want to weigh the returns available and decide which investment combined the highest return with the amount of risk you were willing to take.

> **Bond Tip**
>
> Investing in a U.S. Treasury issue or a highly rated agency bond versus a bank certificate of deposit is a question of what you want to do with the interest. With a bank CD, the interest compounds and is paid at maturity. Bonds pay interest semiannually so you must reinvest it to earn "interest on interest." However, if you want the interest to spend, bonds are the way to go.

Investing in a bond mutual fund does not accomplish the same goals as buying an individual bond. Both strategies add the diversification of bonds to your portfolio, but only owning an individual bond will offer any assurance that at some future date, the bond's maturity, you will receive your principal back. Bond mutual funds fluctuate with market conditions and the value of your shares will rise and fall based on how well the fund manager predicts market shifts. At any appointed future date, you may not be able to redeem your shares for the same or a higher price than you paid.

Buy-and-Hold Motives

There are several motives for owning bonds. One is to make money with the investment. Another is to diversify your portfolio against the stock market's more aggressive nature. The closer you get to retirement, more of your portfolio should be shifted into the stability of bonds and out of the unpredictable swings of the stock market.

Owning individual bonds or bond mutual funds will accomplish both of these goals; however, owning a bond mutual fund does not offer the same degree of predictability when it comes to making money that owning an individual bond does.

The other consideration, however, is that owning a bond index fund gives you the diversification of owning multiple bonds with one investment. Owning individual bonds puts you at some risk of not being diversified by holding the small number of bonds that most individual investors can afford to own.

Trading Motives

Trading bonds is obviously done with making money as the primary motivation. If an investor can make enough to overcome the costs of trading (broker commissions, taxes, research, and so on), it can provide a profitable way to invest in bonds.

Where Bonds Are Traded

New bonds are issued by a governmental entity or corporation and sold through stockbrokers with the exception of U.S. Treasury issues, which can be bought direct. Once a bond is in the hands of an individual owner, it can be sold to another individual just like shares of stock on a stock exchange.

Where to Find Bonds

Previously issued bonds can be bought though stockbrokers who often carry an inventory of bonds for clients. A small number of bonds are listed in major daily newspapers and *The Wall Street Journal*.

The New York Stock Exchange lists the most corporate bonds of any exchange and recently received permission to expand its listings from 1,000 to over 6,000 corporate bonds. The exchange has a new trading system just for bonds, which will make it easier for investors and stockbrokers to find a bond to fit their particular needs.

Market Place

The New York Stock Exchange operates a bond-trading room where bonds are bought and sold in an auction format just like stocks on the main exchange floor.

The bond market in general is a network of brokers who specialize in bonds or have part of their business focused on the bond market. Bonds are sold by connecting buyers and sellers via a computer network. Some brokers carry bonds in inventory for sale to clients. They make a market in certain types of bonds and you may get a better deal, commission-wise, from a broker selling out of their inventory.

The Least You Need to Know

- The Efficient Market Theory says bonds are priced closest to their true value thanks to highly efficient markets.

- Active and passive investment styles describe the amount of involvement in the account by the investor or bond fund manager.

- Keeping investment expenses low is one way to give yourself a chance for investing success.

- Bonds trade in the secondary market through a system of brokers who specialize in buying and selling bonds.

Chapter 3

Risks and Concerns of Bond Investing

In This Chapter

- Interest rate wrecks
- Danger of default
- Watch out for inflation
- Protecting against risk

To the uninitiated, bonds may seem about as risky as putting money in your savings account. No risk there, right? Except if you remember the saving and loan crisis of a few decades back, when hundreds of institutions went belly up as the real estate market collapsed. Depositors got their money back and your savings account is perfectly safe now, but the point is you need to set aside any idea that all bonds are safe.

Bonds must be safer than the stock market, most people reason, and they would be correct with the proper cautions in selecting bonds. Not all bonds are created equal, as we've seen so far, and that inequality in structure and backing changes the quality of the bond's risk profile.

Because bonds range from the most secure investment you can make to one of the riskiest; you have many choices when it comes to finding bonds that match your financial goals and fit your risk profile. The key is matching your needs and expectations with the proper bond that doesn't require more risk than necessary to meet your goal.

Are Bonds Risky?

Compared to stocks, most investors consider bonds a safer, less volatile investment. However, they do carry their own set of risks. As with any investment, the smart investor understands the risks and finds those bonds that match his risk comfort level.

There's Risk Everywhere

The reality of investing is that it comes with risk. The issue for investors is being comfortable with the amount of risk relative to the potential reward. A large amount of risk for a small potential reward is a bad investment. Bond investors must know the risks they face to assess the risk-reward balance.

The risks for bond investors will vary depending on whether you plan to trade bonds on the secondary market or want to hold them until the bonds mature. Risks that affect the market value of bonds are important to traders, but less so (or not at all) to investors who plan to hold the bond until maturity. Other risks, such as the risk of default or credit risk, are important to both the trader and the buy-and-hold investor. Even if your strategy is to buy and hold bonds until maturity, you should be aware of those risks affecting traders, since your plans may change and you may need to sell your bonds before maturity.

Bond Tip

The bond market is no different from the stock market when rewarding and punishing risk takers. The more risk involved in an investment should always mean a higher potential of suffering a loss and the possibility of experiencing an extraordinary gain.

Risk of Time

Long is more risky than short. That is a fundamental fact you need to understand about bonds. The longer the maturity, the more years the bond faces the possibility of bad things happening. You will notice in bond prices that longer maturing bonds usually carry a higher coupon than short-term bonds.

Yield Curve

The yield curve is a term you will hear frequently when the subject of interest rates is discussed.

The yield curve is the acknowledgment of the higher risk of long-term debt instruments and their higher interest rates. There are times when, for a variety of reasons, the yield curve is inverted and short-term rates are higher than long-term rates. Many analysts believe this is one predictor of a coming recession.

In the normal bond market, long-term bonds pay more than short-term issues. The reason is that many things, most of them bad, can happen between when a bond is issued and when it matures at some distant future date. Interest rates change, inflation can go up, the bond issuer can fall on hard times jeopardizing its ability to repay the bond—all of these events, and more, make for greater risks in holding long-term bonds.

This additional risk is why holders of longer-maturing bonds demand a higher return for that risk. The decision for investors is to balance their need for return with their tolerance for risk. If you have a low tolerance for risk and stick with short-term issues, you'll give up the potentially higher returns on longer-term bonds.

Bond Tip

One way to tap the higher yields of longer-term bonds is with a bond mutual fund or exchange-traded fund that has a large percentage of its investments in longer-term issues and the remainder in intermediate and short-term issues.

Inflation Risk

Inflation is a silent tax that eats away the purchasing power of your investments. It is particularly dangerous to bondholders because it erodes the purchasing power of the cash payment they receive and the value of the principal.

Long-Term Dangers of Inflation

A rise in inflation is especially dangerous for mid- and long-term bondholders. As the purchasing power of the dollar declines, so does the value of your bond. The fixed payment feature of a bond means each payment is worth less in a rising inflation environment. For long-term bondholders, 20-plus years of inflation can greatly diminish the purchasing power of the face value of your bond.

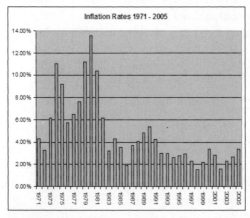

Average annual inflation rates from 1971 to 2005. Information from the Bureau of Labor Statistics.

From the chart, which notes average annual inflation rates from 1971 to 2005, it's clear that inflation has been a terrible force in our economy. However, even when it is relatively mild as it has been for the past decade, it still eats away at the value of a dollar. An inflation rate of 3 percent annually for 20 years will reduce the purchasing power of the face value of a $1,000 bond by almost half.

The price of a newly issued, long-term bond anticipates a rate of inflation and it is built into the price. The purchaser (or lender, if you will) expects a high return to compensate for inflation so the bond will deliver a positive real rate of return. The issuer (the borrower) knows the bond will be repaid in inflated dollars that are worth less than today's dollars so they don't mind paying a higher rate.

If both have anticipated the correct rate of inflation for the life of the bond, everyone wins. However, if the assumption was 3 percent inflation and it actually jumped to 6 percent, there is a big problem.

Bond Tip

The Federal Reserve Board's Open Market Committee meets eight times a year to set key interest rates. They use higher rates to cool an inflationary economy and lower interest rates to stimulate a lagging economy.

Inflation Protection

You can protect yourself from inflation by not buying long-term bonds; of course, this means giving up higher returns. You can choose a middle position and look at mid-term bonds, which give you a better return than short-term bonds, but don't have the exposure of long-term bonds.

You can also buy inflation-protected bonds—the TIPS, and I Bonds from the U.S. Treasury offer returns tied to the rate of inflation. For more information, see Chapter 5.

Interest Rate Risk

Changes in interest rates are the single most important risk factor for bonds, especially mid- and long-term bonds.

How Important Is the Risk?

Changes in interest rates drive the bond market. Short-term bonds don't react strongly to changes because they mature quickly and the market reprices new bonds at the new interest rates. Mid- and long-term bonds, on the other hand, are jerked around by interest rate changes.

The absolute illustration of this is the change in a bond's price relative to interest rates. When interest rates go up, bond prices go down and when rates are dropping, bond prices are rising. The math behind this is explained in Chapter 8.

Think of it as looking in the mirror at your home mortgage. If you knew mortgage interest rates were going up, you might want to lock in a long-term mortgage at today's lower interest rate. If rates do go up, you made a good decision. Now think about the lender who made the loan to you. The lender locked up their money for 30 years at an interest rate lower than what they could have lent it for today. In the world of long-term bond investing, you are the bond lender. If you buy a 30-year bond at 5 percent and one year later interest rates are 7 percent, you are stuck with a poorly performing bond.

You can sell the bond on the secondary market at a discount (loss) or you can hold on and hope interest rates come back down. In either case, you are a victim of interest rate risk for long-term bonds. This is why it is important that the return on a 30-year bond should be higher than the return on a 10-year or a 1-year bond. If it is not and all other factors such as creditworthiness are equal, the 30-year bond is not a good deal—you are taking too much risk for not enough reward.

Here's a look at how changing interest rates and maturities affect a bond's market value (the original bond has a face value of $1,000 and a 6 percent coupon):

Interest Rates

Maturity	4%	5%	6%	7%	8%
1 year	$1,019	$1,010	$1,000	$991	$981
3 years	$1,056	$1,027	$1,000	$974	$948

Maturity	4%	5%	6%	7%	8%
5 years	$1,089	$1,043	$1,000	$959	$920
10 years	$1,162	$1,077	$1,000	$930	$866
30 years	$1,346	$1,154	$1,000	$876	$775

This table illustrates the relationship between interest rates, maturity, and bond value. When interest rates equal the coupon rate, the bond's value equals its face value. However, when market interest rates are higher than the bond's coupon rate (6 percent in this illustration) the value of the bond falls, and the longer the term, the more it falls. If interest rates rise, your bond is worth less. How much less depends in large part on how much time remains until maturity.

The table shows that a 1-year bond at 6 percent coupon rate drops $19 in value ($981) when interest rates go to 8 percent. However, the 30-year bond with 6 percent coupon rate drops $225 in value ($775) when interest rates rise to 8 percent. This works the other way, too. If interest rates fall your bond value must rise, and in this situation it works out better if you are holding a long-term bond. The table shows that a 1-year bond will rise $19 when interest rates drop to 4 percent ($1,109), but skyrocket up by $346 for a 30-year bond ($1,346).

Bond Tip

The table also illustrates the difference time has on bonds. Notice the difference in how much more the 30-year bond changes when compared to the 1-year bond. Whether interest rates rise or fall, the longer term of the bond magnifies the impact on the bond's price.

Falling Rates a Problem, Too

There's no pleasing the bond market. Rising interest rates are a problem, but so are falling interest rates. If you need the income from bonds for living expenses (as in retirement), falling interest rates will mean bonds earn less and when existing bonds mature you may not be able to reinvest the money at the same level of return.

This is another case where playing it too safe can make it hard to reach your financial goals. If you are uncertain about interest rates and keep your investments in short-term bonds, you may find they don't generate enough return to meet your needs. As rates fall (remember 2000–2002), you have lower return options for your investments. Taking a slightly longer-term risk would have actually been the smarter choice, because you would have received a higher return.

> **Bond Tip**
>
> Many financial advisors like the mid-term bond. In fact, the 10-year Treasury note was so attractive it became the standard measuring stick for other issues.

Credit Risk

A bond is a loan, and there is always the risk that you won't be paid. Checking the creditworthiness of the borrower is one way to lower this risk. The creditworthiness of the borrower also relates to the interest the bond pays.

Credit Check

The creditworthiness of a bond issuer plays a role in the coupon rate of the bond. Top-rated bonds pay less because the risk of default is lower, while bond issuers with shaky credit have to pay a higher coupon rate to attract buyers. Like all risk categories, you must be compensated for buying bonds that are not highly rated credit risks.

Fortunately, you don't have to check the references of bond issuers before you buy—several private companies make a business of doing that for you. These companies rate most corporate and municipal bond issues based on the issuers' financial ability to repay the bond. This is not just a one-time shot, but an ongoing process that re-evaluates the issuer to ensure that circumstances haven't changed that would jeopardize its ability to repay the bond.

The most important indicator of a bond's potential to default is its ranking by the three most recognized bond-rating services. Moody's Investors Service, Standard & Poor's, and Fitch, Inc. are the premiere bond-rating services. If a bond is not rated, you should pass on it.

The three companies study bond issuers and rate them on their creditworthiness. Here is an explanation of their rankings. Note the grading system is arbitrary within the different grades. For example, Moody's Aa grade is the same as the Fitch and S&P grades of AA.

Investment Grade—Highest Grade

These bonds carry only the smallest degree of risk. These are the best-quality bonds backed by the issuer's high capacity to meet financial obligations.

Moody's—Aaa
S&P—AAA
Fitch—AAA

Investment Grade—High Grade

These are high-quality bonds by all standards; however, their margin of safety may not be as large as the highest-grade securities.

Moody's—Aa
S&P—AA
Fitch—AA

⊗ Upper Medium Grade

These bonds have attractive investment attributes. Bonds may feel the effects on economic changes more than higher-grade bonds. However, principal and interest are considered adequately secure and the issuer retains strong repayment capacity.

Moody's—A
S&P—A
Fitch—A

Medium Grade

The bonds have adequate capacity to pay, but may suffer from adverse economic conditions.

Moody's—Baa
S&P—BBB
Fitch—BBB

Bond Tip

The three bond-rating services have much more to say about their ratings than the brief paraphrased summary reported here. For more complete descriptions, visit their respective websites. You can find their web addresses in Appendix B.

The rating services go on down for several grades, however you would be well advised to avoid bonds below Medium Grade, as the risk becomes harder to know. Experienced bond traders who can read between the lines may find great opportunity in lower-rated bonds; however, it's not a good place to start—the risks are high.

What Causes Default

You don't have to worry about U.S. Treasury issues defaulting (if that happens, we're all in deep trouble). However, every other type of bond carries some degree of risk of default.

The reality is that you are most at risk when purchasing corporate bonds. Municipalities do default on bonds, but not as often as corporations do. Corporations default for all the commonsense reasons you might think: they run out of cash when coupon payments are due, the company may be forced into bankruptcy because of economic or market pressures, or for any of the other dozen reasons businesses fail. Sadly, your corporate bond may default because of corruption and greed that have brought more than a few companies down in recent years.

Municipalities are businesses, too, and if revenue (taxes) falls short of projections for whatever reason, the community may stop paying on its bonds. Historically, investment-grade municipal bonds have a much lower default rate than corporate bonds with the same rating. If you play the odds, municipal bonds, after U.S. Treasury issues, are the safest from default, but they're not without risk.

Bond Tip

There have been some major municipal bond defaults. Fitch published a study in 2003 that showed from 1980 to 2002 there were 2,339 municipal bond defaults worth $32.8 billion.

This is why sticking to top-rated bonds is important. While no guarantee of payment, a top rating gives you some assurance that the issuer has the financial capacity to meet obligations. Not all bond issues are rated. It costs to have an issue rated by the services. However, you should avoid bonds that are unrated. You have no way of judging the credit-worthiness of bonds unless you are a professional analyst and are willing to spend months performing an independent analysis.

Red Flag

There are scams in the bond industry just like there are scams anywhere there is money. Be very careful of offers for bonds that pay high returns with "virtually no risk" or some similar offer. There are no high returns with no risk in investing, only in scams to take your money.

Other Types of Risk

It may sound like investing in bonds is nothing but risk; however, you need to know all the traps before wading into this market. The fixed coupon and maturity makes bonds subject to market whims and variations. Risks present a challenge for bond-holders to overcome, and a certain amount of risk adds to the potential return as we have seen.

Call Risk

Most municipal and many corporate bonds have call provisions. Call provisions allow the issuer to repurchase the bond before the maturity date. Some call provisions state certain dates the bonds can be repurchased, while other call provisions leave it to the discretion of the issuer.

The risk to the bondholder is that an issuer will likely exercise the call provision when interest rates drop and new debt at a lower rate can refinance the bonds. For the bondholder, this means you lose a bond that is selling at a premium (because the coupon rate is higher than market interest rates) and you will have to reinvest the proceeds in a bond that pays less than the original bond.

Call provisions in bonds should be worth something, so you should be paid slightly more in the coupon rate for having the call risk hanging over your head. Of course, if interest rates climb, it is unlikely the issuer would call the bond.

Reinvestment Risk

Reinvestment risk relates to call risk, and it occurs when a bond is called or it matures and you receive the face value. Reinvestment risk is the danger that interest rates will be lower than the coupon rate on the bond and you will earn less than before. If an issuer calls your bond as explained, it is almost certain that you will face investing the proceeds at a lower interest rate.

This risk is particularly troublesome for people who count on income from bonds for living expenses during retirement. If interest rates are low, bond coupons on new issues will be low also, and buying higher-coupon bonds in the secondary market will require paying a premium. Neither of these choices is particularly attractive.

Bond Tip

Owning bonds with varying maturity dates is one way to work around interest rates that are frequently changing. If all of your bonds mature around the same time and interest rates are low, you are stuck. Spreading maturities over several years allows you the opportunity to reinvest them at different rates—some higher and some lower.

Liquidity Risks

The bond market is the largest market in the world—much larger in dollar value than the stock market. Yet you may find it difficult to buy and sell individual bonds.

Unlike the stock market, the bond market is home to many issues that rarely trade. These bonds are bought, usually in large lots, by institutions (insurance companies, pension funds, and so on). You can find bonds that are actively traded in the secondary market where buyers and sellers meet, but don't assume that every bond falls into that category.

The most active market is in U.S. Treasury issues, and there is a very liquid secondary market. There are listed corporate bonds that trade daily. On the other end, there are issues that rarely trade and can be expensive to buy or sell. Chapter 4 discusses the mechanics of trading bonds and why you want to avoid thinly traded issues.

While you can buy U.S. Treasury issues in units of $1,000, other bonds often start at $5,000 and go up. Add to that a standard trading unit may require a minimum of $25,000 and you can see this is not a market for dabblers. Trading bonds as a way to profit from market swings is best left to those with years of experience. For most individual buy-and-hold investors, liquidity is not a risk, because the intent is to hold the bond to maturity.

To limit liquidity risk of long-term bonds, stick with well-known issues that have a proven secondary market.

The surest way to beat liquidity risk is to do your bond investing through a mutual fund or exchange-traded fund. These professionally run pools of capital are highly liquid investments that let you get into and out of the bond market almost instantly. For more information on bond mutual funds, see Chapter 9.

Bond Tip

Before you set your heart on a bond, find out what the secondary market for the issue looks like. If it is active, you are more likely to get a better price than in a slow market. It will make a big difference in what you pay.

Tax Risk

Congress and the IRS have tweaked the tax code to the point of incomprehensibility; however, there's still more work to do. One change that pops up from time to time is to eliminate the federal income tax exemption on income from municipal bonds. If this were to happen, it would change the value of municipal bonds considerably. The odds of this are very slim, but it illustrates the possibilities.

Other changes may not be so direct. For example, changes in the tax structure of how investments are treated (capital gains, dividend income, and so on) could make bonds less (or more) attractive when compared with other products.

For example, preferred stock is primarily bought for its dividends. If income tax on dividends was eliminated or reduced, investors might consider shifting investments out of bonds and into preferred stock. Income from corporate bonds is subject to federal and state income tax. If the tax on dividends were eliminated or reduced further, investors might shift money out of bonds and into preferred stock for the greater after-tax return. This is an extreme example, but changes in tax policy can have an impact across many product types.

Bond Fund Risk: One or Many

Bonds are typically longer-term investments; however, bond fund managers often buy and sell bonds to get the best yield. This turnover may produce a risk not found in owning individual bonds.

Common sense tells most investors that diversification is the key to reducing risk—and in most cases that is the right answer. However, bonds are not like other investments and so not all of the usual rules apply the same way.

For example, if you ask most investors whether it is safer to own a broadly diversified stock mutual fund or one stock, they would say the mutual fund. Better to own 100 stocks than one stock. One hundred stocks would not all falter at the same time.

However, for bonds it may not be that easy. The reason is that similar bonds all move in the same direction at approximately the same velocity in reaction to the same change. Owning one bond or one hundred bonds wouldn't significantly change your risk. To achieve diversification, you'll want to own bonds of different maturities and different types (corporate, municipal, and Treasury). If you own a bond, you know what it will pay each year and what it will pay at maturity. Owning more bonds won't change those facts.

Red Flag

AAA-rated bonds (the highest grade) with the same maturity will move about the same in response to an interest rate change. Owning one or ten won't change the risk or improve your return. You could substitute one AAA-rated bond for another and not change your risk. That's not necessarily true for lower-rated bonds or high-yield bonds. You cannot count on their returns tracking as closely.

The bond mutual fund works differently. The fund manager is constantly buying and selling bonds, looking for the best yield. When interest rates begin to rise, all the bonds in the fund fall in value. This drives down the value of the fund and its market price.

If interest rates fall, the manager must replace maturing bonds with lower-interest issues, which reduces the overall return. Since a bond fund never has a fixed return or maturity like an individual bond, it is squeezed both ways. Clever managers can work all of this out, and bond funds are convenient ways for individuals to invest.

The Least You Need to Know

- Bonds are considered safer than stocks, but carry their own set of risks.
- Inflation is the risk that future dollars will lose purchasing power.
- Bonds are very sensitive to interest rates.
- Stick with top-rated bonds to protect against the risk of default.

Chapter 4

Buying and Selling Bonds

In This Chapter

- Different markets for different bonds
- Four market parts
- Trading bonds
- How you buy and sell bonds

If you want to buy 100 shares of Microsoft, you follow a procedure that involves contacting your stockbroker and placing the order. If you want to buy 100 shares of IBM, the process is identical as is the process to buy shares of stock listed on any stock exchange. The process doesn't change because you are buying this stock as opposed to that stock. Not so in the world of bond investing, which makes it more complicated for individual investors to participate in the bond market. The market for U.S. Treasury issues is different from corporate bonds and municipal bonds. Buying and selling in these markets is different in part because the bonds are different.

Navigating these markets requires an understanding of how each differs from the others and what you must know to participate in a profitable manner.

Understanding the Bond Market

Bonds are sold to individual investors two ways: at issuance (the primary market) and in the secondary market. However, it is more complicated than that simple statement. Depending on the type of bond, the transaction may be easy and inexpensive or more difficult and expensive.

How Bonds Are Different

Buying and selling listed stocks is a simple commodity service, meaning any licensed stockbroker can perform the service for you, the only difference being the quality of that service and price. You can buy or sell any listed stock with relative ease because there is a ready market and a sophisticated system that matches buyers and sellers. Although buying an *initial public offering* of a stock may be limited to certain favored clients, it is not impossible to be in on the ground floor when a company first issues its stock to the public. Anytime you want to know the price of a stock, that information is readily available from a number of sources.

def•i•ni•tion

> **Initial public offering** is the first time a stock is offered to the public for sale on the open market (stock exchanges).

The world of buying and selling bonds doesn't work this way. Depending on the type of bond you are interested in, buying one at issuance should cost you nothing in commissions and may or may not involve a stockbroker. If you want to sell your bond before maturity, you may or may not need a stockbroker and you may or may not pay a commission. If you want to know the price of your bond before maturity, that information may or may not be readily available. If this seems very confusing, welcome to the world of bonds.

Bond Liquidity and Transparency

Two issues of concern before we move further into the mechanics of buying and selling bonds are liquidity and transparency. These are important because they affect how hard or easy it is to sell different bonds and remind us that they are part of the risks of investing in bonds discussed in Chapter 3.

Liquidity refers to how easy or difficult it is to convert an asset (in this case a bond) into cash. If you want to sell your bond, how hard or easy will it be to find a buyer and what will determine the price? Unlike common stocks, bonds may not have a ready market so finding a buyer willing to pay your price may not be easy.

Transparency refers to how easy it is to get pricing information about bonds. Some bonds, such as those corporate bonds listed in major daily newspapers and *The Wall Street Journal*, are very transparent. Other bonds that trade infrequently and through the over-the-counter market have no transparency to the retail investor. You are at the mercy of stockbrokers who will include their markup or commission in the price they quote you. This means two brokers could easily quote two different prices for the same bond.

Bonds Are Big

The bond market is huge. There are trillions of dollars tied up in bond debt. For the individual investor, however, the important number concerns how dominant institutional investors are in the bond market. By some estimates, individual investors hold about 40 percent of the market value of corporate equities (stocks), but only directly hold 7 percent of the total market value of debt instruments. Since institutional investors dominate the market with 93 percent of the holdings, it is little wonder that the systems and procedures are designed to accommodate their needs.

Pricing systems for tracking the secondary market are designed for large investors who may trade blocks of bonds valued at $1 million or more at a time. These systems are not available to individual investors, and even most stockbrokers don't have access to them because of the cost.

The lesson for the individual investor is you will always pay a premium in the secondary market unless you can trade in large amounts of $100,000 or more.

> **Bond Tip**
>
> Don't let the high thresholds stop you from investing in bonds. Individual bonds can still be good investments. The small investor will always pay slightly more than the large institutions—that's just a fact of the market.

The Primary Market

When a bond is first issued, it is said to trade in the primary market. When you buy a bond in the primary market, there is no commission or markup because the issuing organization pays the stock-broker (for corporate and municipal bonds).

Primary Market—U.S. Treasuries

New U.S. Treasury bonds are sold at auction or by other direct means, which is a completely different method from corporate or municipal bonds. You can buy bonds directly from the Treasury by establishing a Treasury Direct account with the Federal Reserve Bank. This simple process can be done online. You can also buy Treasury issues through many banks or other financial institutions that will charge a fee that usually runs $50 or less.

Either way, the term "auction" is somewhat misleading. An auction does occur every Monday for Treasury bills, for example, but most individuals don't actually bid. They submit a "noncompetitive" bid, which means they will accept the interest rate established by the Treasury Department after the true auction. Institutional investors looking to buy $500,000 or more in T-bills (one T-bill equals $10,000) bid an interest rate for that week's offering. After all the institutional bidders who submitted acceptable bids have been awarded the amounts they wanted, the Treasury sells the remaining T-bills to individuals who submitted noncompetitive bids at the average of the accepted bids.

Treasury bonds and notes are also sold in a similar manner at auction, however the times are less frequent than T-bills.

Primary Market—Corporate and Municipal Bonds

Corporate and municipal bonds follow a completely different path from Treasury issues. These bonds are not sold directly to retail investors, but are offered by an investment bank acting as an *underwriter*. For large issues, several investment banks may work together in what's known as a *syndicate* to buy the bonds from the issuer and sell them to the public. In an initial offering of this type, the syndicate offers the bonds to the public at the same price. This is important because there is no markup in price or commission. The bond issuer pays the selling costs. Buying corporate or municipal bonds at issue assures individual investors that they are paying the same price as everyone else. As we'll see in the discussion of the secondary market, that's seldom the case.

def•i•ni•tion

An investment banking firm **underwrites** or guarantees the sale of the bond issue, almost always buying the whole issue outright if possible. The investment bank then sells the bonds to large institutional buyers and, in some cases, part of the issue may go to retail brokers for sale to the public.

A **syndicate** is formed by a group of investment banking firms to underwrite a bond issue too large for one firm to manage on its own.

The Secondary Market

Once a bond has been bought at issue, any subsequent buying and selling of the bond is done in the secondary market. This market operates "over-the-counter" for the most part, but individual investors have no direct access to this market—all purchases and sales are through stockbrokers.

Secondary Market—U.S. Treasuries

The secondary market—buying and selling previously issued Treasury bonds—is a highly liquid and transparent market. Prices of previously issued bonds are quoted in financial newspapers such as *The Wall Street Journal*, so investors know what the bonds are worth in the open market. The cost to buy and sell previously issued bonds becomes the stockbroker's commission. You can't buy and sell previously issued Treasury bonds directly; you must use a stockbroker. Since investors can know the price of the Treasury bond they are interested in buying, the difference is the commission charged by the stockbrokers.

Secondary Market—Corporate and Municipal Bonds

As transparent as the secondary market is for U.S. Treasury issues, the secondary market for corporate and municipal bonds is mostly hidden. With some exceptions, it is difficult for individual investors to discover the price of many corporate or municipal bonds. There is no ready network to find prices of many previously issued corporate or municipal bonds. Some websites list trades in corporate and municipal bonds, which is helpful information but not the same as what the bond will trade for today.

Part of the problem is that many bonds, especially issues that have been in the market for a number of years, may not trade for extended periods. Research indicates that only around one percent of all outstanding bonds trade on any given day and less than 30 percent of all outstanding bonds trade at all during a single year. With the exception of the bonds listed in daily newspapers, it may be difficult, if not impossible, for individual investors to discover the price of specific bonds unless the bond is actively traded. Several websites report trades of bonds, list prices, and other information. However, investors must completely understand the bond market and how it prices issues to use these sites. In addition, you must know specific information about the bond issue to find it among the several million outstanding bonds. See Appendix B for more information on these sites.

Trading Bonds

Buying and selling bonds in the secondary market is not as easy as trading stocks; however, it is done every day by investors. The mechanics are different and may not be comfortable for everyone familiar with stocks.

What You Should Know About Bond Prices

When you are buying bonds in the secondary market, the price includes a *markup*, which is the stockbroker's profit. This is the usual situation if you are buying a bond out of the broker's inventory. Many brokerage houses hold bonds in inventory and sell them to customers. If the firm does not have the particular type of bond you are looking for, it may have to acquire the bond from another brokerage house. In this case, you will probably pay a premium on top of the markup. You should ask for full disclosure of pricing before you make a bond purchase. Not all brokers charge the same for handling bonds, and your chances of earning a profit on any investment—bonds included—increase when you keep expenses low.

def•i•ni•tion

The **markup** on a bond's price is the difference paid by the purchaser between the retail price and wholesale price, which is the price in the interdealer market. Markdown would be the difference received at the retail level on the price of a bond off the wholesale price.

A Bond Is a Bond

When shopping for a bond on the secondary market, remember that bonds that have the same rating and maturity will perform the same when market conditions change. For example, an AAA-rated, 10-year bond from one utility district will react to market conditions the same as another AAA-rated, 10-year bond from another utility district.

When you go to a stockbroker to buy a bond, it is usually not important to specify which utility district's bond you want to buy—unless one is in your state and that is important for the tax-free income. Bonds with the same rating and maturity are virtually interchangeable when bought in the secondary market.

Finding a Broker

Most large stockbrokerage companies handle bond trades as well as stocks. If you have a relationship with a stockbroker, ask about their bond capabilities. Firms that offer the best service to investors carry an inventory of bonds for their clients. If they don't carry bonds in inventory, you will pay more because they will have to acquire the bond you want from another broker and pay a markup, then add their markup before giving you a price. Bond brokers should disclose markup if asked, as well as commissions and other fees.

A knowledgeable broker can be very helpful in your bond investing; however, watch what you pay in fees. Brokers' fees, commissions, and markups are for the most part unregulated. This means they are free to charge what they will, and since in many cases you can't know the bond's price in advance, you are at their mercy.

The Spread

As in stock over-the-counter markets, the secondary bond market trades on the bid-offer spread. This two-price market describes the seller's price and the buyer's price. The difference between the two prices is the spread and the broker's fee for handling the trade. The bid is the price you will get to sell a security (stock or bond), while the offer is the price you must pay to buy the security (stock or bond). As you might conclude, the offer is always the higher of the two prices.

The factors that affect the size of the spread in the bond market relate to the amount of risk the broker must incur to own the bond in inventory. The greater the risk, the larger the spread, which is consistent with an understanding of risk and reward. Three specific risks that affect the spread are:

- Creditworthiness—The higher the bond's credit rating the smaller the spread, while a lower credit rating means a larger spread.
- Price volatility—The more volatile the bond's price, the larger the spread.
- Liquidity—The more liquid a bond, the smaller the spread, while less liquid bonds will have a larger spread.

Research Tools

Individual investors are at a disadvantage when it comes to researching specific bond issues. Unless you know a particular company or municipality issue, it may be difficult to find out more about the bonds themselves.

Standards for Identification

When corporate or municipal bonds are issued in the primary market, they come with a disclosure statement that lists all the details of the offering. Once the bond begins trading in the secondary market, those details are often hard to find, especially for the individual investor.

There are steps to improve the communication to individual investors. However, because they make up such a small percentage of the bondholders, reforms will almost always favor institutional investors. One step that will help individual investors is the requirement that all corporate, municipal, and mortgage pass-through bonds now have a nine-digit CUSIP (Committee on Uniform Security Identification Process). A CUSIP makes a bond issue searchable out of the thousands of issues on the market. This lets investors with the right access track the bonds when they are bought and sold. Unfortunately, that access is still very expensive, but some brokers who have the service will provide investors with pricing information.

Bond Tip

With individual investors holding so little of the bond market (seven percent or so), don't look for many radical changes in your favor. However, the Internet, as it has done with everything else, brings a flood of information that was never available before.

Online Pricing

Given the thousands of bond issues and the fact that most bonds are owned by institutions, it's not surprising that public information on individual bonds may be difficult to find. Treasury issues and some corporate issues are regularly reported, as are representative municipal issues. However, if you want to find out specific trading information on a specific bond issue that isn't regularly reported, you may find that information difficult to come by.

In Appendix B are websites that offer pricing information on recent bond issues that have traded. It is important to note that what these sites often report is the last trade for the bond. This may or may not be what the bond will trade for the next time a sale is made. Unlike most stocks, which trade frequently during the day, many bonds make no trade at all for lengthy periods.

Since bonds that have the same credit rating and maturity will generally respond to market conditions the same way, you can get an idea from watching trading activity of these bonds for clues. What you must factor in is the markup by the broker and any commission you pay.

Reading Bond Tables

Bond tables are shorthand reports of trading activity found in newspapers and online. This information is helpful in your research and easy to understand once you figure out all the columns of numbers and abbreviations.

Corporate and municipal bond listings are usually reported by newspapers in an identical format, while Treasury and federal agency quotes are slightly different. Note that prices are quoted as divided by 10. For example, IBM in the quote below closed at 88.37. If you multiply that by 10 you get 883.70, which is the actual price. A corporate bond quote might appear in a newspaper like this:

Bond	Cur Yld	Vol	Close	Net Ch
IBM 5½ 25	6.2	100	88.37	-0.25

This quote tells you that it is for an IBM bond with a coupon of 5.5 percent or paying $55 per year interest on a $1,000 bond. It matures in 2025. Volume was 100 bonds and the last transaction was for $883.70, a decline of $2.50 from the last close. The current yield is 6.2 percent and is found by dividing the current coupon ($55) by the closing price ($883.70).

Few daily newspapers carry municipal bond quotes. *The Wall Street Journal* and *Barron's* report a limited selection of municipal bond quotes. You can find more information on both corporate and municipal bond trades at www.investinginbonds.com.

Treasury issue quotations might appear in the newspaper like this example:

Rate	Maturity Mo/Yr	Bid	Asked	Chg	Ask Yld
5.000	Mar 10n	105:22	105:23	5	3.77

coupon

This is for a Treasury note with a 5 percent coupon and a March 2010 maturity (the n tells you it's a note). Most quotations include closing bid and asked prices and are quoted in "32s." The bid in this quote is $105^{22}/_{32}$ or $1,056.87, while the asked quote is $105^{23}/_{32}$ or $1,057.19. The change indicates the bond closed up $^{5}/_{32}$ over close of the previous session. The asked yield is the yield to maturity. The asked price is used because that's the price buyers pay. (The asked price is the same as the "offer" price noted in the discussion of the spread earlier.)

It is important to note that prices for Treasury issues quoted in newspapers are for large institutional purchases. Individual investors will pay more for their purchases and receive less when they sell.

The Least You Need to Know

- Different types of bonds are available in different markets—knowing where and how bonds trade is key to successful bond investing.
- Individual investors have their best buying opportunity when bonds are initially issued—called the primary market—because they pay no commission.
- You need a knowledgeable stockbroker to trade bonds in the secondary market.
- It is difficult for individual investors to find current pricing on bonds in the secondary market.

Chapter 5

U.S. Treasury and Agency Bonds

In This Chapter

- U.S. Treasury bills, notes, and bonds
- Treasury Inflation Protection Securities
- U.S. savings bonds
- Agency savings bonds

In the best of all worlds, reasonable taxes and fees collected by the federal government (and all other governmental units) would be enough to pay for the services it provides. This actually happens occasionally, although it is usually because the economy is especially robust rather than through exceptional management by the federal government. When taxes and fees don't cover the cost, the government must borrow the difference. During times of war or economic slowdown, the difference can be substantial. The U.S. Department of Treasury is responsible for raising the necessary funds and does so by issuing Treasury notes, bonds, and other debt. Because these issues are considered the benchmark for safety, investors from all over the world buy them as a safe repository for their assets.

Agency bonds are not issued by the Treasury Department, but by various agencies within the federal government, mainly those involved in housing and student loans. They have many of the same characteristics as Treasury bonds plus some that are uniquely their own.

U.S. Treasury Issues

Debt issued by the U.S. Treasury comes in several forms and is often referred to generically as Treasury issues, because some of the securities are not strictly bonds. However, they all have the same general features.

Safety of Principal

U.S. Treasury issues are considered the most secure investment on the market because they are backed by the full faith and credit of the U.S. Government. This means the assets, resources, and taxing authority of the U.S. Government stand behind the guarantee of repayment of principal. This security is unique in the investment world and makes Treasury issues suitable for any portfolio.

You should not confuse Treasury issues with risk-free investing, however. Like any fixed-rate security, Treasury issues are subject to the adverse affects of interest rate changes. For example, if you buy a five-year Treasury note that pays 5 percent interest and subsequently interest rates rise to 6 percent, your note will be worth less because it does not pay the current market rate. See Chapter 8 for more information on how interest rate changes affect bond prices.

Bond Tip

Foreigners own some 53 percent of the outstanding debt of the United States. Some believe that this makes us vulnerable in a crisis where a large number of these foreign debt holders would cash in their I.O.U.s. Others argue that this is nonsense because it presumes the economic crisis will be worse here than other places, which is not likely.

Demand for Treasury Issues

The demand for U.S. Treasury issues is huge, due to their security and the liquidity of the secondary market. Foreign investors, both individuals and institutions, buy large amounts of each new Treasury issue. This gives them a stable return on their assets, which is especially important in economies that are subject to upheavals in the value of the domestic currency.

For U.S. investors, the safety provides institutions with a low but guaranteed return where preservation of capital is more important than growth.

For individual investors who are particularly risk averse, there is no safer haven than U.S. Treasury issues.

Tax Issues

U.S. Treasury issues pay a relatively low return, thanks to the high degree of security they afford. However, a key feature that somewhat offsets this low return for some taxpayers is that the income is free from state and local income taxes. You still must pay federal income tax on the interest payments. However, for residents in states with a high personal income tax, Treasury issues and some federal agency issues may be attractive options.

> **Bond Tip**
>
> If you live in a state with a low personal income tax rate (or none), the returns on Treasury issues become less appealing. In these situations, investors' primary motivation is security rather than yield.

Sold at Auction

All U.S. Treasury bills, notes, bonds, and TIPS are sold at auction, although at different times. On the first Wednesday of February, May, August, and November, the Treasury publishes a tentative multi-month schedule of upcoming auctions.

You can find the tentative schedule for auctions at www.savingsbonds.gov and a schedule of auctions with firm dates. However, auctions are only firmly scheduled a few days before they happen. You can sign up to be notified by e-mail when auctions are scheduled.

U.S. Treasury Bills *Not really for individual*

U.S. Treasury bills, or T-bills, are not true bonds since the securities have maturities ranging from 4 to 26 weeks. Most definitions of bonds require a minimum one-year maturity. However, T-bills fall into the Treasury issue category and can be useful to individual investors in certain circumstances.

Sold at Discount

T-bills are sold at auction in $1,000 denominations. As mentioned in Chapter 4, the auctions happen every Monday. You can participate directly by opening an account with the Federal Reserve (it's a one-page form) or have a bank or other financial institution act for you.

The T-bill is one of a very few U.S. Treasury issues that are not sold at face value; rather, they are sold at a discount. The amount of the discount determines the interest the T-bill pays. For example, an investor might buy a $1,000 26-week T-bill for $970. At the end of the 26 weeks, the investor redeems the T-bill for the full $1,000. The difference of $30 is the interest earned for the period, which works out to a little over 3 percent.

Uses for T-Bills

T-bills are very short-term investments and, coupled with the high level of security, pay a low interest rate. They may not be very practical for many individual investors. As a place to park cash, they don't pay enough to compete with money market mutual funds, bank money market accounts, or bank certificates of deposit.

However, there are circumstances where the immediate rate of return is secondary to security or where you need a place to put a large sum of cash temporarily. For example, the executor of a will may find that parking a large amount of cash in T-bills until the estate is settled is a prudent way to avoid any chance that the principal amount is compromised.

Likewise, you could suddenly come into a large sum of cash through an inheritance or some other means and need some time to decide what to do with the windfall. Rather than tie up the money in multiple CDs at multiple banks to stay under the $100,000-per-account FDIC protection, you could drop the whole chunk in T-bills with no worries about the principal.

Red Flag

T-bills offer top-notch security, but their yield in normal markets is quite low. You can earn a much better return with short-term bank CDs or money market funds that pose little risk because of their short term.

U.S. Treasury Notes

Treasury notes are bonds with maturities of more than 1 year, but no more than 10 years. This middle range of maturities makes notes very popular with investors who want some of the benefits of longer-term bonds, but don't want the risks going out more than 10 years.

Sold at Auction

Like T-bills, Treasury notes are sold at auction in denominations of $1,000. Notes have maturities of 2, 3, 5, or 10 years. They carry the same repayment guarantee of all Treasury issues, making them very secure. Notes pay interest every six months. You can buy them directly from the Treasury or through financial institutions for a small fee.

The 10-year Treasury note is considered the benchmark for investment security and is often used as the proxy for calculating the "safest return" you can earn. The auction dates for notes are:

- Two-year notes—monthly
- Three-year notes—February, May, August, November
- Five-year notes—monthly
- Ten-year notes—February, *March, May, *June, August, *September, November, *December

  The Treasury reopens previously issued bonds and sells additional amounts on these dates. The reopened security has the same maturity date and interest rate; however, it has a different issue date and usually a different purchase price.

Treasury notes offer a fixed coupon rate and maturity. The price the notes sell for and the interest rate is established at auction. If the interest rate established at auction is higher than the coupon rate, the price paid at auction will be slightly discounted so the interest rate yield and coupon rate match.

Likewise, if the interest rate set at auction is lower than the coupon rate, the price at auction will be slightly higher than face value to make the two rates match.

The math for these adjustments is explained in Chapter 8. However, the rule to remember is that as interest rates move up, the price of the bonds moves down and as interest rates fall, the price of the bond rises.

> **Bond Tip**
>
> Treasury notes, especially those in the midrange of maturity, are extremely popular because they strike a balance between the high yields of longer-term bonds and the safety of shorter-term investments.

Uses in Your Portfolio

Treasury notes, especially in the intermediate range, work well in any portfolio that needs a steady source of income and absolute safety. Like all Treasury issues, they are free from state and local income taxes, so their relatively low yields are more attractive to people in states with high income tax rates.

Even with their relatively low returns, Treasury notes may beat other investments that are much riskier when you consider the after-tax return. If you could earn 4.5 percent on a Treasury note, it probably doesn't make any sense to take a risk for a 4.75 percent return on another investment that doesn't have the same security and tax advantages.

U.S. Treasury Bonds

The U.S. Treasury halted issuing 30-year bonds for a number of years, but popular demand drove them to resume issuing the security in February 2006. The long-term bond was the benchmark of debt investing for many years.

Sold at Auction

Treasury bonds pay interest every six months and come in $1,000 denominations. They are sold at auctions, which the Treasury sets every year, usually in February, May, August, and November. Like other Treasury issues, you can buy them directly from the Treasury or through a financial institution for a small fee.

Bonds follow the same purchase procedure as detailed for notes with the interest rate and price set at auction. Because bonds have the longest term of any Treasury issue, they typically pay a higher rate because of the added interest rate risk investors assume with long-term, fixed-income investments. (See Chapter 3 for a discussion of the relationship between length of the bond's maturity and interest rate risk.)

There are times when shorter-maturity notes may pay as much or more than longer-term bonds. This relationship is called an inverted yield curve and it signals a time when investors should avoid taking the extra risk of long-term bonds because the safer shorter-term issues pay more. Investors should be aware of the extra risk in bonds and be sure the bonds pay additional interest to compensate for the risk.

Uses in Your Portfolio

Treasury bonds may pay a higher rate of interest than other Treasury issues due to their longer term. However, for most investors seeking a higher return, bonds may not pay enough for the risk over time.

Institutional investors who need to match long-term liabilities to assets find the bond particularly attractive.

Market Place

The 30-year bond was so popular that after it was discontinued, investor demand brought it back. The demand, however, was from institutional investors who have different motives for long-term investing than individual investors.

TIPS for Inflation Protection

Treasury Inflation Protection Securities (TIPS) are bonds that adjust to the rate of inflation, which addresses one of the major risks affecting bond-holders.

A Different Approach

TIPS may not qualify under strict definitions of a bond, which is usually thought of as a fixed income investment with a certain face value at maturity. TIPS offer investors neither a fixed interest payment nor a certain face value at maturity (although it will never be less than the original face value).

TIPS interest payments and eventual face value are tied to changes in the *Consumer Price Index*. The security pays a fixed rate of interest; however, the principal adjusts to the Consumer Price Index (CPI), commonly known as the measure of inflation. If the index rises in a period of inflation, the principal is adjusted upward. Since the fixed interest rate is now applied to a larger principal, your semiannual interest payment is increased.

def•i•ni•tion

> The **Consumer Price Index (CPI)** is the primary measurement of inflation. It measures a basket of goods and services considered vital to everyday life and marks the increase or decline in these goods over time. The Bureau of Labor Statistics issues the CPI and other inflation measurements monthly.

For example, assume you owned a $1,000 TIPS with a stated interest rate of 3 percent, and the CPI rose 2.5 percent during the year. To calculate your new interest payment, you would first adjust the principal by the inflation rate of 2.5 percent, which gives you $1,025 ($1,000 × 2.5% = $1,025). You then apply the annual interest rate of 3 percent and get $30.75 ($1,025 × 3% = $30.75) as your new interest payment.

If the CPI drops, the principal is reduced and your interest payments are lowered. However, at maturity you will receive either the original face value of the bond or the inflation-adjusted value, whichever one is greater. The U.S. Treasury website provides inflation index ratios that will let you calculate the change to the principal from changes in the CPI.

Sold at Auction

TIPS are sold at auction in the same manner as notes and bonds in $1,000 denominations with maturities of 5, 10, and 20 years. The auctions are:

- 5-year TIPS in April and October*
- 10-year TIPS in January, April*, July, and October*
- 20-year TIPS in January and July*

    *These are reopenings like notes.

You can buy TIPS directly from the Treasury or through a financial institution for a small fee. Like all Treasury issues, TIPS interest is exempt from state and local income taxes.

Uses in Your Portfolio

TIPS are exceptional investments because they provide a guaranteed protection against inflation that is not found in any other of the usual inflation hedges such a stocks or hard assets like gold or real estate. Bonds, including other Treasury issues, build an expectation of inflation into the interest rate. When inflation exceeds this expectation, bonds can suffer loses. TIPS protect against this situation and outperform conventional issues.

TIPS' fixed interest rate will be less than conventional Treasury bonds of the same maturity because of the risk premium for inflation that bondholders expect with conventional issues. This means that if inflation is flat or declines, return on a TIPS would be less than if you had purchased a conventional Treasury issue. Although you will not receive less than the face value of the TIPS bond at maturity, the initial lower interest rate and possibly reduced principal before maturity means your return will be lower than the same investment in a comparable Treasury issue. If you have to sell the TIPS bond before maturity, you may not get the full face value.

For example, a five-year Treasury note and a five-year TIPS issued in the same month might have a 2 percent difference in the interest rate established at their respective auctions. For illustration purposes, suppose the note had a 4 percent interest rate and the TIPS had a 2 percent interest rate. The additional 2 percent interest on the note reflects a premium to the bondholder for inflation risk. The TIPS bond carries no such premium because its principal will adjust to changes in the CPI. If inflation rises more than is expected during the five-year life of the two bonds, the TIPS will outperform the note. If inflation does not rise or declines, the note will outperform the TIPS.

Red Flag

Investors, especially retirees counting on a steady income, should not have more than 30 percent of their holdings in TIPS. If you see no threat of inflation soon, that percentage should be less. The small return you could potentially earn from TIPS in a low-inflation environment will hurt your cash flow.

Retirees, who are especially vulnerable to the negative affects of inflation, find TIPS a comforting hedge without the investment risks of stocks or other counters.

Unlike other bonds and fixed-income investments, the inflation risk you take with owning TIPS is that it will be flat or decline. You won't lose any of your principal if you hold the TIPS to maturity, but you will not receive the income you may have expected. Investors should also be aware that the inflation adjustment to the principal is taxed and may want to consider holding TIPS in retirement accounts where the tax liability is deferred. It is always a good idea to discuss investments with tax implications such as TIPS with a qualified tax advisor to determine the best way to hold the securities for your personal situation.

I Bonds for More Inflation Protection

I Bonds are another inflation-protected security from the Treasury that has many of the same features as TIPS, but with some significant differences and benefits.

Buy Them Direct

Unlike previously discussed Treasury issues, you do not buy I Bonds through the auction system. I Bonds are sold directly by the Treasury, through various financial institutions and even through some payroll savings plans. The bonds are sold at face value and come in electronic and paper form. You can buy paper I Bonds in $50, $75, $100, $200, $500, $1,000, $5,000, and $10,000 denominations. The electronic version can be bought to the penny at amounts over $25 ($50.35, for example). You are limited to $60,000 per year in purchases of I Bonds. (See the U.S. Treasury website for details. You'll find its web address in Appendix B.)

The Treasury announces new fixed interest rates for I Bonds in May and November, and those rates apply for bonds issued during the following six months. At the same time, the Treasury announces an inflation rate adjustment. These two rates are combined in a formula to produce a composite rate, which is what the I Bond earns for the next six months. The bonds increase in value on the first of each month and compound semiannually. Note that you do not receive semiannual interest payments as you do with regular Treasury bonds. The interest accrues in the bond until it is redeemed.

The I Bond pays interest for 30 years. You can cash in the bond anytime after the first 12 months. However, if you cash it in before five years, you'll lose the last three months of interest as a penalty. The interest is deferred from federal income taxes until you redeem the bond, which makes I Bonds attractive to hold in taxable accounts. Once you pass the five-year holding limit, there is no penalty for withdrawal before the 30-year maturity date.

> **Bond Tip**
>
> I Bonds pay no interest until you redeem the bonds, much like zero-coupon bonds. However, you don't pay any taxes on the accruing interest until the bonds are redeemed, which differs from zero-coupon bonds.

Education Benefit

I Bonds have a special benefit if you have children who may be attending college in the future. I Bonds qualify for the Education Bond Program, which means all or part of the interest may be exempt from federal income taxes. If you redeem the I Bond in the same year you pay for qualified higher education expenses or contribute to a state tuition plan, interest in a like amount from your bond that is redeemed in the same year is exempt from federal income taxes. At certain income levels, the exclusion is reduced and finally eliminated. Check with the Treasury website for current income levels where reductions begin.

Uses for I Bonds

I Bonds are attractive inflation-protection securities that work well in regular accounts since the interest is tax-deferred until the bond is redeemed. This allows the bond's value to grow and it adjusts to any rise in inflation, thanks to the inflation-adjustment component of its interest rate. Like TIPS, the I Bond will not perform as well as regular bonds during periods of low or no inflation. With I Bonds, you will always get at least the face value at redemption no matter what the inflation situation and no matter how many years you have held the bond.

The education benefit of the I Bond is a nice plus, but there are better ways to save for a college education that involve slightly more risk and offer a better return. Still, if you are looking for an absolutely safe way to save for college that is protected from inflation and may be tax-exempt, I Bonds may be an answer.

Series EE Savings Bonds—One More Choice

EE Savings Bonds are similar to I Bonds, but have some interesting features. Savings bonds are often thought to be gifts for grandchildren rather than serious investment tools. It is a mistake to overlook this alternative investment.

Same, but Different

EE Savings Bonds and I Bonds share many common features:

- Both are exempt from state and local taxes.
- They share the same credit guarantee of all Treasury issues.
- They defer income tax until the bonds are redeemed.
- They earn interest for 30 years.
- Individuals can buy up to $60,000 worth each year subject to some conditions.

EE Bonds are also part of the Education Bond Program, so like the I Bond, all or part of the interest income may be excluded from federal taxes if you have qualifying higher education expense in the same year you redeem the bond and meet the income test.

EE Bonds have a one-year holding period before you can redeem them, and you will lose three months of interest if you cash in the bonds before five years. The bonds earn a fixed rate of interest that is set by the U.S. Treasury.

Bond Tip

Although you can buy EE Savings Bonds in paper form, it is usually a better idea to buy them electronically. The chance of losing a paper bond outweighs the attractiveness of holding a piece of paper.

If you buy bonds electronically, you pay face value and can purchase in any amount over $25, even to the penny. Paper EE Bonds are sold at 50 percent of face value and the Treasury guarantees they will double in value in 20 years.

Uses for EE Bonds

EE Savings Bonds can be used in your retirement planning, to finance college, and, yes, as birthday or graduation gifts. Because you can always redeem them at face value and without penalty after the holding period, EE Bonds are a highly liquid and stable investment. However, their interest rate will be slightly lower than regular Treasury issues.

> **Red Flag**
>
> EE Bonds and older issues of savings bonds don't have a "maturity" date as such. Most of the savings bonds continue to earn interest for up to 30 years, but you can hold them as long as you want. However, if it is not earning interest, there is little point in hanging on to an old savings bond.

U.S. Agency Bonds

The federal government sponsors several enterprises and agencies that work in important areas of the economy. The main function of these entities is to lower the cost of capital to specific areas of the economy. They do this by issuing bonds, and this is where investors can profit.

Government-Sponsored Enterprises and Agency Bonds

There are two organizational forms you should know about: U.S. government agencies and government-sponsored enterprises (GSEs). Both are active issuers of bonds and the two organizational types are similar in their offerings, but there are some differences. The major distinction is that some of the GSEs are privately owned companies, while others are government agencies.

Although most of the GSEs and agency bonds do not carry the "full faith and credit" of the U.S. government, they are considered just a small step below U.S. Treasury issues in safety. There is an implied support of these issues, since most play a critical role in the economy. Investors assume the government would not let any of these GSEs fail, making the bonds very safe. The major credit-rating agencies usually give the bonds their highest rating. The major GSE issuers are involved in making housing more affordable by stabilizing and encouraging the home mortgage market and loans for college students. There are some other agency issuers, but they tend to only offer very large products to institutional investors and account for only a small portion of the total agency bonds issued. For individual investors, the most active issuers are:

- The Federal Home Loan Mortgage Corporation, or Freddie Mac—Created as a quasi-government agency, it has spun off into a private company that trades on the stock exchange. Freddie Mac buys pools of mortgages, guarantees them, and sells participations. This helps stabilize the secondary market.

- The Federal National Mortgage Association, or Fannie Mae—This is also now a publicly traded company, which borrows money in huge amounts and uses it to purchase mortgages from lenders. It also issues mortgage-backed securities.

- Student Loan Marketing Association or Sallie Mae—If you are familiar with financing a college education, chances are good that you know Sallie Mae as the largest guarantor of student loans. Investors buy into a pool of these loans and benefit from the guidelines that prevent eliminating student debt in bankruptcy and stricter collection procedures.

Note: the three previous GSEs are privately owned companies. The following issuers are either regional banks or direct agencies of the U.S. government.

- Federal Home Loan Banks—This is a banker's bank that lends money to financial institutions, which in turn make mortgages.
- Federal Farm Credit System—This agency provides credit to agricultural businesses, including farms and farm-related industry.
- Tennessee Valley Authority or TVA—This massive electrical generating project and the accompanying development it brought to some isolated areas of the South is a big bond issuer.

There are other GSEs, but these are the biggest issuers. You can find pricing on these securities in *The Wall Street Journal* and other financial publications.

Market Place

A number of U.S. government agencies issue bonds, including the Small Business Administration, the U.S. Postal Service, and many more. Many of these issues are taken by large investors. The bulk of securities issued by agencies are for the housing market.

Housing-Related Securities

Bonds or securities issued by GSEs are different from regular bonds because many are structured around the housing market and home loans in particular. Although some of the less well-known GSEs are involved in other segments of the economy, the housing market is the focus of the top issuers.

Constructing securities around home mortgages is more complicated than it may seem on the surface. Investing in these issues, while considered relatively safe, shouldn't be attempted until you understand the product. Some of the securities have a $25,000 minimum, which is not a sum most people want to experiment with in their investing.

Mortgage-backed securities come in several forms, and you should study individual issues carefully before investing. The two basic types include:

- Mortgage pass-throughs
- Collateralized mortgage obligations

Mortgage Pass-Through Securities

Mortgage pass-through securities allow investors to participate in the housing market by owning part of a pool of home mortgages. As homeowners pay their monthly mortgage note, investors receive a pro rata share of the principal and interest of the mortgage pool. Investors in these securities receive a payment each month or quarterly, depending on the type of security, rather than the usual twice-yearly schedule. If the security is held to maturity, the investor does not receive the full face value, because they have been receiving partial principal payments during the life of the security.

Mortgage pass-throughs pay investors based on the cash flow through the pool of mortgages. Some mortgages are paid on time, month after month, while other mortgages may be paid off due to a sale or refinancing after only a few years. Because the investor doesn't know in advance how many loans will be paid off early, the income from many of these types of loans fluctuates each pay period.

An obvious risk is that the homeowners may pay off their mortgage early and you will not receive the full benefit of the interest payment. This may happen en masse if interest rates fall and a number of people refinance at lower rates. This is essentially the same risk as bondholders who have their bonds called early. The investor in both cases must reinvest the funds at lower interest rates.

Collateralized Mortgage Obligations

Collateralized mortgage obligations (CMOs) are a much more complex security that takes a pool of mortgage pass-through bonds and/or actual mortgages and creates a multiclass security. CMOs pay income to various maturity classes called tranches. A CMO could have from two to a dozen or more tranches. Each tranch has a different maturity, so some investors get paid off early, while others are paid off later in the life of the CMO. There are a number of variations on this concept, all designed to meet specific investment objectives.

Uses for Agency and GSE Bonds

Government agency and GSE securities are very safe investments that may be attractive to investors looking for a higher yield than straight Treasury issues. However, like all investments, you should be certain you understand the securities completely before investing.

These securities have much going for them, especially if you plan to hold on to them, rather than trade in the secondary market. They are safe, pay more than U.S. Treasury issues, and come in a broad array of configurations.

On the downside, there is not as much liquidity in the secondary market as you will find for Treasury issues. Be certain of your investing goals before devoting resources to these products.

You can buy most of the bonds with $1,000 minimums, although some securities require up to $25,000 minimum. You should have a financial professional who is very familiar with these issues help you determine which is right for your particular situation.

As with any investment, there are risks. Many agency bonds have a call feature, which means you may have the bond called away during periods of falling interest rates. You should limit your investment in agency and GSEs to 25 percent of your fixed-income portfolio as a matter of diversification.

The Least You Need to Know

- U.S. Treasury issues are the safest investment you can make because there is no credit risk.

- Income from U.S. Treasury issues is free from state and local taxes, making them attractive in states where there is a high personal income tax.

- TIPS and I Bonds provide a measure of protection against the effects of inflation.

- Agency bonds offer a higher yield, good safety, and a variety of configurations.

Chapter 6

Corporate Bonds

In This Chapter

- Corporate bond fundamentals
- Risks of corporate bonds
- Types of corporate bonds
- Corporate bonds in your portfolio

Corporations issue bonds to pay for large projects, such as new plants and equipment, acquisitions, and other major investments. Companies can borrow money through a bond issue for longer terms than usually available from commercial lenders. Interest rates and other conditions of the loan (bond issue) may also be more favorable to the company than those demanded by banks or other lenders.

In the world of bond investing, corporate issues, as a group, are the most risky. You can find highly rated corporate bond issues, but there are many issues that fall below the level of prudent credit-worthiness. Why would an investor buy such a bond? The only reason to take investment risk is for the expectation of a higher reward. Corporate bonds that fall below the top ratings of Moody's or S&P are considered speculative. (See Chapter 3 for more information on credit ratings.)

The corporate bond market is huge and surprisingly liquid. The New York Stock Exchange has a bond trading floor that will facilitate trades on over 6,000 corporate bonds of companies listed on the exchange. This increases its recent level of about 1,000 bonds and adds transparency to the process. This expansion is waiting for SEC approval of NYSE's new bond-trading platform.

Daily trading volume in the corporate bond market exceeds $24 billion. The total value of outstanding corporate bonds is well over $4 trillion. Institutional investors such as insurance companies, mutual funds, pension funds, banks, and others dominate the corporate bond market. Individual investors are not locked out of the corporate bond market and may find the rewards worth the risk.

Market Place

The bond market is huge—much bigger than the stock market in dollar value. However, because some 93 percent of the outstanding bonds are owned by institutional investors, most of us hear more about the stock market where the individual investor has more influence.

Corporate Bond Fundamentals

Corporate bonds offer the investor comfortable with more risk the opportunity to earn significant rewards. Investors who understand the risks invest in corporate bonds for their potentially attractive yields, steady income, and safety.

Uses of Bonds

Corporations use bonds to finance a variety of projects including new facilities, acquisitions, and other needs requiring low-cost, long-term financing. Bonds are often the least expensive way for companies to borrow money. This creates an opportunity for investors to become long-term lenders to corporate clients.

Bond Tip

Bonds should show negative correlation to stocks—that is, as stocks react to economic news, bonds should either not react or move the opposite direction. A perfect negative correlation would mean bonds would move in the exact opposite direction of stocks. That seldom happens, but bonds are less volatile than stocks, which helps stabilize your portfolio.

Corporate Bond Description

Corporate bonds sell in denominations of $1,000 or $5,000. A minimum trade for most corporate bonds is five units, which could mean a minimum $25,000 investment for some issues. As noted in the following sections, corporate bonds come in a variety of configurations—some of which are not individual investor friendly.

A bond is a legal debt obligation of the corporation to repay you the principal by a certain date (maturity) and interest at the terms described. Corporate bonds generally pay a higher rate of interest than a comparable Treasury issue or municipal bond. One of the reasons is that interest from corporate bonds is not exempt from any income tax—not federal, state, or local. You generally pay ordinary income tax on the interest from corporate bonds unless you hold them in a tax-deferred retirement account. Obviously, at maturity the repayment of the face value is not taxed since this is a return of principal and not earnings.

Another reason corporate bonds pay higher interest rates is that they are generally more risky than Treasury or municipal bonds. You can find numerous corporate bond issues that receive top ratings by the three credit agencies; however, as a group, their creditworthiness is lower. Corporations have no taxes to rely on for generating income to pay off the bonds. Some corporate bonds are secured by hard assets such as real estate, but most are not, and the bondholder is relying on the company to generate enough income to pay its obligations.

Red Flag

The main indicator of a corporate bond issue's risk is its credit rating. The organizations that rate bonds monitor them and the company after the bonds are issued. It is possible for a bond issue to be downgraded (or upgraded) by the credit agencies after it has issued. A negative change will impact the market price of the bonds. However, it does not change your annual interest payment or the face value of the bond you receive upon redemption.

Interest Rate Variations

Corporate bonds pay interest on the principal amount for the life of the loan in most cases. However, there are several different ways corporate bonds are structured that allow an alternative to the traditional interest payment method.

Traditional bond interest payments are made semi-annually for the life of the loan. Most corporate bonds still follow this structure. Investors receive two payments that together make up the coupon rate of the bond. For example, a XYZ corporate bond for $1,000 with a 6 percent coupon rate makes two $30 interest payments per year.

Some corporate bonds offer a floating or variable interest rate. The interest rate is pegged to an index such as short-term Treasury notes or a money market indicator. Periodically, the bond's interest rate adjusts according to the index or indicator used. While offering some protection against interest rate risk, these bonds often start at a lower interest rate than fixed-rate bonds. The reason is that fixed-rate bonds build in a factor for interest rate risk, which is not present in floating-rate bonds.

> **Bond Tip**
>
> Corporate bonds offer investors a wide variety of options including interest rate calculations. Your financial professional can help you determine which type of bond works best for your financial situation.

Zero-coupon bonds may be more familiar to many investors. These bonds pay no interest, but sell at a deep discount to face value. The interest earned is realized when the bonds mature and are redeemed for full face value. More detailed information on zero-coupon bonds follows in Chapter 10, since these bonds are not particular to corporate issuers.

Who Issues Corporate Bonds?

Although any corporation can issue bonds (as long as it meets the regulatory guidelines), some types of businesses are the most frequent issuers. These include:

- Industrial or manufacturing companies
- Transportation related companies
- Utilities

- Conglomerates
- Financial service companies
- Some foreign companies

All of these business types have at least one thing in common: they are *capital intensive*. This means their business requires an extraordinary amount of capital to operate.

def•i•ni•tion

Some businesses are **capital intensive**, meaning they require much more capital to operate than others. Businesses such as transportation (airlines, railroads, and so on) need lots of money for equipment, fuel, personnel, and so on. That is why they are said to be capital intensive.

Certainly, other businesses issue bonds, but those that must buy and operate expensive equipment or raise large sums of money (like financial services companies) face a challenge in keeping financing costs as low as possible. Bonds are often a solution and hard assets with long useful lives lend themselves to collateralizing bonds.

Bonds: Secured or Not

Bonds are legal debt owed by the corporation. Some bonds are unsecured debt, while other bonds are backed by some form of collateral. Like any debt, the company pays higher interest on unsecured bonds.

Bonds in Repayment Priority

Bonds represent a legal debt by the corporation. In the event of bankruptcy, bondholders will be repaid before stockholders receive anything. In all debt situations, there are various priorities of debt. Debt that is secured by assets has claim on those assets before any other debtor. Once secured debtors are paid off, unsecured debtors have claim on remaining assets.

Some bonds command a higher priority in the repayment schedule than other bonds do because of the collateral associated with the issue. It is rare in a bankruptcy that every debtor comes out with all of the money owed them, which is why risk-averse investors prefer secured bonds that have a higher priority claim on assets for repayment. If a company is bought by another company, the purchasing company either assumes all the debt, including the bonds, or the bonds are repaid by being called early.

Types of Bond Security

Security for bonds ranges from none to hard assets such as real estate and equipment. Unsecured bonds pay a higher coupon rate because of the higher risk that there will be nothing left to repay them in the event of a bankruptcy. Secured corporate bonds are less risky because of the collateral attached to them, but pay a lower coupon rate. Some of the major bond types are:

- **Debentures**—Unsecured bonds are called debentures. These bonds offer repayment based on the cash flow and general economic health of the issuing company. If the company is a large, well-established company, with a high credit rating, the risk of default is not high. However, bonds from companies with shaky credit and troubled finances may be highly speculative (risky).

- **Subordinated debentures**—Subordinated (also called junior) debentures are bonds that fall behind secured bonds and debentures in the repayment schedule. Only after secured bonds and debentures have been paid do subordinated debentures get paid. Because they are so far down the line, these securities command a high coupon rate to compensate for the added risk.

- **Mortgage-backed bonds**—These bonds are secured by deeds to real estate, equipment, or other hard assets. There are several varieties of mortgage-backed bonds that represent debt against the asset at various levels, such as: a first, second, or third lien; junior; and so on. It is important to know where the bond falls in the pecking order to determine when it will be paid in the event of a default. Too far down the line and there may not be any money left.

- **Equipment trust certificates or bonds**—
  These securities are most used by airline and
  railroad companies to buy equipment. Title
  to the equipment bought with the bonds is
  held by a trustee until the debt is repaid.

- **Guaranteed bonds**—Guaranteed bonds
  are backed by a third party, kind of like co-
  signing a loan. You see this most often when
  a subsidiary of a large corporation has its
  bond issue guaranteed by the parent. The
  guarantee buys a slightly lower interest rate.

> **Bond Tip**
>
> Although as a group corporate bonds
> are more risky than U.S. Treasury or
> municipal bonds, you can find conserva-
> tive investments in this bond sector also.

Call Provisions in Bonds

Many corporate bonds contain a call provision
that allows the issuer to call or redeem the bond
before its maturity. Call provisions are not investor
friendly and you should receive a premium in the
coupon rate to compensate for the added risk.

Defining Call Provisions

Many corporate bonds (and municipal bonds) have
some form of call provision in the indenture. A call
provision allows the issuer to call or redeem the

bonds prior to their maturity. A company might want to call certain bonds for several reasons; however, the primary reason usually is that interest rates have fallen. The company can redeem the bonds and refinance the debt, often with a new bond issue, at a lower interest rate, saving money.

For investors, bonds that are called represent a loss of future income—specifically the difference between what the original bonds paid and what they must now accept in lower interest rates. The risk, described in Chapter 3, is known as reinvestment risk. For example, if you owned a bond with a coupon rate of 6.5 percent and it was called because interest rates had dropped to 4 percent, you would face a reinvestment loss of 2.5 percent, because that is how much less new bonds earn.

When a bond is called under these circumstances, the bondholder is paid the full face value of the bond, plus any accrued interest. However, that would be less than the market value, since a bond paying 2.5 percent more than the current interest rate would command a premium price in the secondary market. The math explaining how this works is discussed in Chapter 8. The investor loses not only the higher interest payments, but the opportunity to sell the bond for a premium over its face value.

Bondholders have some protection with certain issues that set the call price above the face value of the bond. This means if the company calls the bond, you are paid more than the face value. Some bond issues have a waiting period before they can be called, which is stated in the indenture. This gives you some assurance of income for that period.

Types of Calls

Bonds may have different types of call provisions. If you buy a bond with a call provision, it is important to know exactly what the terms are and under what conditions your bond might be called.

Some industries, such as utilities, may issue partial calls related to certain maintenance and upgrade provisions. Other calls may be tied to financial triggers concerning assets pledged as collateral.

One of the most common forms of call provisions is the sinking fund. A company will establish a fund that must be paid into each year out of earnings to retire the bonds. Part of this structure requires that a certain amount of bonds be retired each year. Bonds are often chosen by chance for retirement. Sinking funds are good for those bondholders who aren't called because it helps make the company more financially secure and less likely to default. However, if your bond is called you may suffer a loss (not of face value, but of interest income) that is inconvenient.

Special Types of Corporate Bonds

Corporate bonds come in some unique configurations that offer investors different possibilities when it comes to choosing a particular type. The two most common types of special corporate bond issues illustrate the flexibility of the market.

Convertible Bonds

Convertible bonds are part equity and part debt. If you own a convertible, you have the right to convert it to a predetermined number of shares of common stock at a predetermined price. It is very much like owning a bond with a stock option.

Convertible bonds state the conversion ratio in the indenture.

The conversion ratio states how many shares you can convert from your bond. The ratio (sometimes called a premium) is usually expressed in one of two ways (assume the bond has a face value of $1,000):

- As a ratio—The bond could carry a conversion ratio, for example 55:1. This means your bond could be converted to 55 shares of common stock. This ratio sets the price per share ($1,000 ÷ 55 = $18.18). This price is higher than the current stock price when the bond is issued. You would only convert if the stock price rose above $18.18 because you could convert your bond to stock for less than the market price.

- As a percentage—The conversion premium can also be stated as a percentage based on the price of the stock at issue. For example, a 50 percent conversion premium means you could convert your bond to a certain number of shares by paying a 50 percent premium over the price of the stock at issuance. For example, a convertible bond issued at a 50 percent premium gives you the option to buy the underlying stock at 50 percent above the stated conversion price. If the stock were selling for $10 per share, you would be able to buy shares for $15 per share ($10 × 50% increase = $15). If the price of the stock rose to $20 a share during the life of the bond, you could convert your bond to shares at the rate of $15 per share or about 67 shares ($1,000 bond ÷ $15 per share = 67 shares approx.).

Either way, you convert your debt instrument (bond) to equity (stock). This may seem like the best of all worlds, because if you don't convert (stock's price falls), you still receive interest payments and return of principal. For investors, this is a critical point. The value of a convertible bond is tied in large part to the price of the underlying stock. If the stock is trading well above the stated price of conversion, your bond is valuable; however, if the stock's price falls or dips substantially, you are stuck with the bond alone.

Because convertible bonds have the potential to return more than an average bond, they pay a lower interest rate than regular corporate bonds of the same rating and maturity. One of the risks you face is that if the price of the stock stays low, your bond will not perform as well as a regular bond and you won't get the stock either. However, the bonds still pay no less than face value at maturity.

Bond Tip

Convertible bonds can skew your portfolio's mix of stocks and bonds because, depending on the stock price, it may act more like a bond or a stock.

There is another risk from what is known as a forced conversion. This happens when the price of the underlying stock rises dramatically. The issuer usually retains a call provision that forces a conversion if the price of the stock goes too high. This has the effect of putting a cap on the appreciation you can enjoy while holding the stock option in the form of a convertible bond.

In effect, there is a floor if the stock does not rise in price (you get your money back at maturity) and there is a ceiling on the appreciation the company will allow before forcing a conversion.

Bond Tip

Convertible bonds are not for the first-time investor. Make sure you thoroughly understand the conversion premium and circumstances of any call provision before making a decision.

Although convertible bonds have their followers, many analysts are not fond of them because they mix debt and equity. If the stock's price is below the conversion price, you own a bond. If the stock's price is above the conversion price, you may own a bond or it may be an equity, depending on how high the price rises.

High-Yield Bonds

Some investors are always looking for a better return and are willing to take extra risk to get it. High-yield bonds fit their need for a fixed-income investment that pays better than regular bonds. High-yield bonds carry credit ratings below investment grade. (See Chapter 3 for more information on credit ratings.) The bonds are often rated several levels below what most solid corporate bonds would score. As a result, they pay a higher coupon rate to compensate for the extra risk.

High-yield bonds are also known as junk bonds, which tells you something about the quality of their credit. This doesn't mean high-yield bonds are automatically bad investments. However, most people invest in bonds for stability and security— two words not often associated with junk bonds.

If you understand the risks and keep high-yield bonds to a small percentage of your portfolio, there's no reason not to consider them. In some cases, you could earn 2 percent or more over investing in investment-grade bonds. There are some concerns you should be aware of:

- High-yield bonds respond to changes in the economy more severely than regular bonds do. The bonds react more like stocks than bonds to many economic changes. This defeats, in part, the purpose of owning bonds, which is to have an asset that does not react the same way as stocks to economic changes.

- High-yield bonds may not pay enough of an interest premium for the risk involved. Investors need to gauge whether the potential reward is worth the risk. If you can buy investment-grade bonds that have a return that is close to high-yield bonds, then why take the extra risk for a small incremental return?

- High-yield bonds can be very illiquid. If you need to sell your bond before maturity, it may be difficult to find a buyer at a price you want to accept. Some high-yield bonds trade very infrequently, making it difficult to get out of a bond early if you need the cash.

- Junk bonds may have a call feature. In most cases, an issuer would call in bonds if interest rates fell and new bonds could be issued at a much lower interest rate. The danger with junk bonds is that the issuing company may have its credit rating upgraded. It can then call in the old bonds and reissue new bonds at a lower interest rate. There are several provisions that favor the issuer, but few for the person buying the bonds.

Corporate Bonds in Your Portfolio

Do corporate bonds have a place in your portfolio? The answer depends on your risk profile and financial goals. Corporate bonds offer some attractive features for your consideration along with some obvious risks.

Where Corporate Bonds Fit

A well-constructed portfolio is diversified by asset class and within asset classes. This means you should consider holding more than one type of bond in your portfolio. Some bond mutual funds and exchange-traded funds help you do this by owning different types of bonds. If you opt for individual bonds or own bonds in addition to mutual funds, you should be aware of the need to diversify by type of bond.

Corporate bonds allow you to participate in various sectors of the economy. You can look for bonds in sectors that are stable (utilities) or bonds in growth areas (technology). The risk factor will vary from sector to sector, increasing or decreasing the yields in much the same way growth stocks are more volatile than established industries. This is important if your investment strategy is buying and selling corporate bonds in the secondary market.

Buy-and-hold investors may be more concerned with stability and income than capital appreciation of the bond's price in the secondary market. These investors may avoid corporate bonds with call

provisions so they can lock in income for a predictable period. They may be willing to give up some
current return for a more certain future of steady
income.

Bond Tip

Owning corporate bonds doesn't have
to be any more risky than you want it
to be. If you are careful and understand
credit risk, corporate bonds fit in just about
every portfolio.

Benefits of Corporate Bonds

As noted previously, corporate bonds, as a group,
are more risky than most other types of bonds.
However, even more conservative investors can
find highly rated bonds that are not so risky that an
investment would keep you awake at night. Higher
yields are one factor that make corporate bonds
worth considering. With a little additional risk
comes a better rate of return.

Because of the large number of new and previously
issued bonds, investors have a good chance of
finding just the issue they need that provides a
reasonable return for reasonable risk.

Note that separate bond issues from the same company may have different credit ratings. A variety
of reasons can influence this situation, including
collateral and other factors. Don't assume that just
because one issue of a company is highly rated all
will be.

Liquidity of Corporate Bonds

Corporate bonds listed on the stock exchanges (primarily the New York Stock Exchange and the American Stock Exchange) are highly liquid in large amounts. The liquidity of smaller trades varies from issue to issue, but corporate bonds are second to only U.S. Treasury issues in the secondary market for ease of buying and selling.

You will need a good stockbroker that understands bonds and the market to execute your orders. Most bonds are still sold over-the-counter, meaning brokers match buyers and sellers. Many brokerage houses sell bonds out of their inventory, while others buy on a wholesale level and resell to investors.

> ### Red Flag
>
> Be cautious when reading bond trades in the newspaper. Those trades are usually for very large lots—up to $1 million at a time. You will pay a significant premium over those prices for a small trade.

Types of Bond Registration

Bonds used to be issued on ornately printed certificates, often with the owner's name on each one. However, bonds have gone the way of stocks and primarily use the registry or book entry system. Under this type of registration, there are no certificates issued. Your ownership is held electronically for you by the stockbroker—much the same as owning stock where the broker keeps track of your holdings. The other types of registration are:

- Registered bonds—Bonds are printed with the owner's name and usually held by the owner. Bonds no longer come with coupons to send in when it is time to collect interest. The issuer's representative sends you checks at the predetermined times and for the face amount when the bond matures.

- Bearer bonds—Bearer bonds have not been issued since 1982. Most people were glad to see the number drop, since the bonds are the near equivalent of cash. Virtually anyone in possession of a bearer bond can cash it for its current market value. There are still bearer bonds in circulation.

Trading Costs

As covered in Chapter 4, buying and selling corporate bonds requires the use of a stockbroker. Many brokers that trade bonds for their clients keep an inventory of bonds that they can match with investors' needs. This cost may be buried in the price of the bond, so it is important to ask your broker for a fully disclosed statement of expenses.

Trading costs for a small order (generally, the minimum order is five bonds) can eat into profit potential very quickly. It is extremely important that your broker fully disclose their charges, so you can compare pricing with other brokers for a comparable bond of the same maturity and credit rating. New issues come commission-free because the issuer pays those costs. If you are interested in a new issue, your broker can get a prospectus for you.

There are other resources listed in Appendix B that will help you find out more about individual issues and the companies behind them.

The Least You Need to Know

- Corporate bonds are the most risky, as a group, of all bonds.
- You pay taxes on all income from corporate bonds.
- Some corporate bonds are backed by hard assets like real estate or equipment, while others are unsecured.
- Call provisions can result in the loss of future income if the bond is called in a market of falling interest rates.
- Junk bonds and convertible bonds are two well-known variations of corporate bonds.
- With proper cautions, corporate bonds can find a role in almost everyone's bond portfolio.

Chapter 7

Municipal Bonds

In This Chapter

- Municipal bond fundamentals
- Types of municipal bonds
- Tax issues
- Insured municipal bonds

The third major category of bonds is radically different from the other two in several major ways we'll explore in this chapter. Although all three share some basic characteristics, they differ widely in important areas such as security, liquidity, tax consequences, and market appeal.

Municipal bonds are a huge market with a value near $2.3 trillion dollars and tens of thousands of different issuers. The largest owners of municipal bonds are mutual funds, money market funds, property and casualty insurance companies, commercial banks, and individuals. Absent from the municipal bond market are the big pension funds and profit-sharing plans that buy heavily into the U.S. Treasury and corporate bond market. These large investors are tax-exempt and have no need for the tax benefits of investing in municipal bonds.

Municipal Bond Fundamentals

Local and state governments, known as *municipalities* for bond purposes, issue municipal bonds to finance projects such as new roads, bridges, and other large construction projects. Other types of municipal bonds may help encourage economic growth.

def•i•ni•tion

In the world of municipal bonds, **municipalities** refers to any state, county, township, city, and so on that issues bonds. It could also be a tax district such as a utility, road, or sewer. Municipal bonds include securities issued by all sorts of government entities and agencies at the state level or below.

The Basics

Most municipal bonds are issued at face value with a fixed coupon rate and maturity. In those ways, they are similar to corporate and U.S. Treasury bonds. Municipal bonds tend to be long term to match the useful lives of the projects they finance (roads, bridges, and so on); however, municipal securities can also be issued for much shorter terms. Bills have maturities of less than a year.

Municipal bonds generally pay semiannual interest payments. Investment-grade municipal bonds are, as a group, safer than corporate bonds, but not as safe as U.S. Treasury bonds. Most issues are rated by one of the major credit agencies and that rating signals the creditworthiness to investors.

Municipal bonds, also known as munis, are sold in $5,000 denominations or multiples of $5,000. *The Wall Street Journal*, some major daily newspapers, and other resources listed in Appendix B, carry bond prices, although these are for actively traded lots of $1 million or more. Prices for small lots will differ.

The most attractive feature of municipal bonds is that the income is exempt from federal income tax and, in most cases, exempt from state income tax in the state of origin. This tax-free income is desirable for individuals in high income-tax brackets and may be worth considering by investors of more modest means in certain circumstances. More about this attractive benefit follows.

Bond Tip

Tax-free income is often a welcome source of cash for retired people who may not have as many deductions (mortgage paid off, for example) as working taxpayers and would pay higher taxes on regular income.

Two Types of Municipal Bonds

Municipal bonds fall into one of two general categories:

- Revenue bonds—These bonds are repaid from revenues generated by the projects funded by the bonds, such as toll roads, rents, and so on.

- General obligation bonds—These bonds are backed by the full faith and credit of the issuer along with the taxing power municipalities have.

You might assume that general obligation (GO) bonds were more secure because of the taxing authority behind the repayment. Theoretically, a municipality could simply raise taxes to meet its obligations for the bonds. However, raising taxes is not automatic. In some areas, there are legal limits to how much taxes can be raised and voter approval may be required. GO bonds still must pass rigorous examination by the rating agencies to garner a good rating.

Revenue bonds are rated on the ability of the project to generate enough money to repay the bonds. The credit rating may be based on economic conditions to the extent they impact the project's ability to generate enough revenue to pay the bond's obligations. Some types of revenue bonds are more risky than others, but this risk is always built into the credit rating.

Calls in Municipal Bonds

Many municipal bonds, like corporate bonds, are issued with call provisions. A call gives the issuer the right to redeem the bond before its maturity. There is often an initial lockout period when the bond cannot be called. This can be from one year to any number of years.

Following the lockout period, the issuer is free to call the bond under the conditions outlined in the indenture. There may be specific dates stated in the indenture or anytime after the lockout. The call must be at par and may be at a premium over par in some cases. Chapter 3 discussed the risks of calls in detail. When buying a bond, be sure you understand if there is a call provision and what the details are. Your stockbroker should quote you a yield to call as well as yield to maturity, since you have to assume there is a possibility the bond will be called before maturity. The yield to call would assume the bond is called on the earliest possible date—also called the yield to worst.

Red Flag

Be sure you understand the call provisions in any bond you buy and be sure there is a premium for the additional risk you are taking by owning a callable bond.

How to Buy and Sell Municipal Bonds

The municipal bond market is huge. There are more issuers and bond issues than most people imagine, which means a virtually unlimited supply of product for investors to explore.

Bonds Are Big

When you look at the numbers associated with the bond market and compare them to the stock market, you might wonder why all the fuss over stocks. The total value of all outstanding bonds is over $21 trillion, more than twice the value of all shares of stock being traded on U.S. markets. U.S. Treasury issues take the largest share of this debt, but municipals account for almost 10 percent. Over 50,000 issuers of municipal bonds have some 2 million separate issues on the market with daily volume exceeding $11 billion.

Even with that level of volume, some issues rarely trade—investors hold on to them to maturity. Actively traded issues are typically owned by mutual funds that may need to adjust their port-folio frequently.

Municipal Bond Prices

A number of factors go into bond prices both at issue and in the secondary market. The municipal bond market is very crowded, so some issuers, especially those that are not as well known to investors, may be forced to enhance their offering to attract buyers. These enhancements include higher yields, discounts off face value, insurance (discussed in the section "Insured Municipal Bonds"), and other measures.

However, the most important factors are the yield and creditworthiness, followed by length of maturity, call provisions, and other special features.

The factors that can change the value and yield of a municipal bond in the secondary market include changes in interest rates (more about this in Chapter 8), changes in credit rating, and supply and demand.

Bond Tip

In many ways, municipal bonds respond to market influences the same way as other bonds. Trading bonds on the secondary market can be more challenging because some issues rarely trade.

Municipal Bond Brokers

Municipal bond brokers belong to the Municipal Rule Making Board (MRMB). Brokers and some banks belong to this organization which self-governs the buying and selling of municipal bonds. The Securities and Exchange Commission oversees the market with regulatory authority. Bonds are only offered through brokers in the secondary market.

Brokers and others that specialize in municipal bonds should have a better knowledge of the market and carry a good selection of bonds in inventory. The municipal market can be complicated and a good broker will help you with product selection as well as executing trades. The MRMB requires that markups and commissions be fair and reasonable, but there are no binding regulations on what those commissions should be. Individual investors trading small lots (five or fewer bonds) will pay a premium to most brokers. Markups that exceed three percent are not unusual, especially for certain bonds that involve extra work for the broker. The broker should disclose all markups in the confirmation paperwork.

Limited Benefits of Diversification

Owning individual municipal bonds requires a different approach to diversification. In most investing situations, diversification protects the investor from large losses by spreading investment dollars among several different opportunities. If one stock falters or an individual bond defaults on interest payments, the others in the portfolio are not likely to follow. In these cases, owning more than one bond offers investors some protection.

When economic forces such as interest rate changes move against bonds, there is not much to be gained by this strategy. Here's why: highly rated municipal bonds will react to market forces in very much the same manner, regardless of the issuer. The largest determinant of bond value and yield are changes in market interest rates. If market interest rates go up, virtually all highly rated municipal bonds will react exactly the same way (their prices will fall). Whether you own 5 bonds or 50 bonds, it won't protect you against this systemic risk.

You can achieve some yield advantage by owning bonds from different issuers in different geographic areas. The supply and demand forces may make bonds in some states more attractive than bonds in other states, which could provide a higher yield; however, it won't offer much protection from rising interest rates. Bond mutual funds accomplish geographic and credit diversification much more efficiently (assuming costs are reasonable). There is more information on bond mutual funds in Chapter 9.

Bond Tip

Don't assume that all your tricks from investing in stocks will work in the bond market. No two stocks are exactly alike, and you can't predict with absolute certainty how each will react to future circumstances. Similarly rated bonds with the same maturity will move in tandem to market changes.

Zero-Coupon Municipal Bonds

Zero-coupon municipal bonds are issued at a deep discount to face value and pay no interest. The investor redeems the bond at full face value at maturity. The difference between the purchase price and the face value is the interest earned. There is a more complete discussion of zero-coupon bonds in Chapter 10.

Tax Issues of Municipal Bonds

Interest income from municipal bonds is generally exempt from federal income taxes. This tax-exempt feature makes municipal bonds attractive to high-income individuals. However, there are other tax implications of buying and selling municipal bonds that you should understand.

Tax-Free Income

Interest income from most municipal bonds is exempt from federal income tax. It is also exempt from state and local taxes if the issuer is in the state where you live, in most cases. These so-called "triple-exempt" bonds are very popular in states with high income tax rates. You should check with your financial professional concerning specific laws in your state that affect municipal bond taxation. Chapter 9 has information on bond mutual funds that invest in these bonds for residents of particular states.

Because of this tax-exempt status, municipal bonds pay a lower rate than similarly rated corporate bonds. The net to the taxpayer in a high marginal tax bracket can be greater, thanks to the tax-free income. For example, an investor with a combined 40 percent federal and state income tax bracket might compare two bonds, one taxable and the other a municipal. Assuming the credit risk and other factors were comparable, here is how the investor might compare the returns:

	7% taxable bond	5% municipal (tax-free) bond
Bond amount	$50,000	$50,000
Interest	$3,500	$2,500
Income tax (40%)	$1,400	$0
Net return	$2,100	$2,500
After-tax yield	4.2%	5.0%

Another way to compare the two bonds is to calculate the tax equivalent yield. This calculation provides you with an "apples to apples" comparison of yields. Here's the simple formula:

Tax equivalent yield = tax-free yield ÷ (1 − tax rate)

Using our example, we plug in the numbers:

Tax equivalent yield = .05 ÷ (1 − .40)

Tax equivalent yield = .05 ÷ .06

Tax equivalent yield = 8.33%

This tells you that a taxable bond would have to return 8.33 percent to equal the return of a 5 percent tax-free bond if your combined federal and state marginal income tax rate was 40 percent.

Using our previous example to test our calculation, if the taxable bond earned 8.33 percent it would earn interest income of $4,165. The tax at 40 percent would be $1,666. Your after-tax yield would be $4,165 − $1,666 = $2,499 or the same (accounting for rounding off) as the yield on the 5 percent municipal bond ($2,500).

It is important for investors to calculate these returns before assuming a tax-exempt bond will always be the best investment. A low marginal federal income tax rate or a smaller spread between what a taxable bond yields and what you get from a municipal bond will erase or diminish the advantage of the muni.

Municipal bonds come in a variety of maturities, so you can find long-term to short-term bonds to match your financial needs. The yields on various maturities will change and may reduce or eliminate the advantage of tax-exempt income.

Red Flag

Do the math. If you are in a low federal income tax bracket and live in a state with low or no income taxes, municipal bonds may be a bad choice for your portfolio. Comparing the after-tax returns and tax equivalent yields will give you the answer.

Other Tax Considerations

Interest income may be exempt from federal income tax liability, but there are several situations where municipal bonds create tax liabilities. Investors can be in for a rude awakening if they aren't prepared for the tax consequences of certain municipal bond transactions. There are situations that produce tax liabilities for investors:

- Alternative Minimum Tax
- Capital gains and losses
- Original issue discount
- Interest deduction disallowance
- Social Security considerations
- State tax treatment
- Market discount
- Taxable municipal bonds

Tax laws are complicated and individual circumstances require a personalized understanding of how they apply to your unique situation. This discussion is a very general introduction to some of the more common tax circumstances. It should not be construed as comprehensive tax advice, which should only come from qualified tax professionals.

Watch Out for Alternative Minimum Tax

The Alternative Minimum Tax (AMT) is a parallel tax system instituted in 1969 to prevent wealthy taxpayers from claiming so many exemptions that they owed no taxes. The AMT eliminates most exemptions and requires certain taxpayers to recalculate their taxes under AMT rules and pay the higher total. Over the years, AMT has not kept pace with inflation and its net has dipped lower in the income pool, grabbing millions of taxpayers the rule was never designed to catch.

For investors, certain municipal bonds are characterized as "private activity bonds" or PABs. PABs are issued to finance certain private activities such as airports, housing, or industrial development activities. When calculating AMT, taxpayers must include income from PABs—in other words, the tax exemption is lost under AMT.

PABs may carry a slightly higher interest rate than regular bonds and may be attractive to investors not subject to AMT. Investors should be concerned that bonds subject to AMT are less liquid in the secondary market. If you are buying bonds in the secondary market, be sure you understand if the bond is subject to AMT or not. Even if you are not currently subject to AMT, be careful that you are not caught as the tax includes more taxpayers each year. Check with your tax advisor before making an investment that may put you at risk for AMT, as the rules for applying AMT are tweaked every year.

Some mutual funds buy PABs to boost their overall yield. There is nothing wrong with this; however, make sure you understand whether the fund does this or not. If the fund does invest in PABs and you are subject to AMT, part of the income you receive will be calculated under that system. The fund is required to disclose their policy on this issue, but you may have to look for it.

Capital Gains and Losses

Investors experience a capital gain or loss when an asset is sold for more or less than the purchase price. There are two types of gains and losses: short term and long term. Long-term gains and losses involve assets held more than one year. Short-term gains and losses apply when the asset is held less than one year.

The interest from a municipal bond is exempt from federal income tax in most cases, but not from capital gains taxes. In the simplest example, if you buy a bond for $5,000 and later sell it for $5,300 dollars, you will experience a capital gain. How long you have held the bond before selling will determine if it is a short- or long-term gain. The same would be true if you sold the bond for a loss, except you would have a capital loss.

It is often more complicated than that, however. The real concern is establishing your basis for tax purposes to determine the size of gain or loss. If you bought the bond at a discount when it was issued (not uncommon), you will have a change in basis (see the following section "Original Issue Discount"). Selling costs and other factors, such as paying a premium for the bond, will adjust your tax basis.

Before you sell a bond, check with a qualified tax advisor to understand how your adjusted basis may affect your tax bill.

> ### Bond Tip
>
> Capital gains and losses can be used to offset other tax liabilities and losses and, in some cases, can be carried forward. However, you should check with a qualified tax professional for clear guidance in your personal situation.

Original Issue Discount

When investors buy an original issue bond at a discount to face value, the IRS considers the difference between the discounted amount and the face value as interest income and it is exempt from federal income tax. However, the original issue discount increases the investor's tax basis in the bond to the face value over time. For example, if an investor buys an original issue bond with a face value of $5,000 for $4,750, the $250 is considered interest income, the same as regular interest except it is collected at maturity when the bondholder will receive the full face value of $5,000.

If nothing changed, the taxpayer would also face a $250 capital gain since the original purchase price was $4,750. However, the IRS uses the $250 to step up the bondholder's tax basis over the life of the bond, so that when redeemed at maturity, the tax basis and the face value are the same: $5,000.

If the investor wants to sell the bond before maturity, there is a formula for calculating the tax basis along the way. Your broker or tax professional can help you make the calculation.

> **Bond Tip**
>
> Original issue discount can be a tricky calculation, especially if you sell the bond before maturity. Thanks to the IRS, nothing is simple about calculating what regular interest is and what a capital gain is. See your tax advisor for guidance.

Interest Deduction Disallowance

Investors can deduct the interest on borrowed money used to finance investments in some cases. However, you are not allowed to take a deduction on your income taxes for borrowed money to buy or hold municipal or tax-exempt bonds. The thought behind this disallowance is taxpayers would receive two benefits: a deduction of the interest expense from the loan and tax-free interest income from the bonds.

This rule doesn't mean you can't have debt while owning municipal bonds. The IRS doesn't expect you to cash in your bonds to pay for a house, so borrowing to finance your residence is allowed and you retain the interest deduction on your mortgage. The rule doesn't generally preclude borrowing that is for activities whose primary purpose is unrelated to investing in municipal bonds.

The IRS has special procedures for individuals and corporations concerning areas where the value of the investment in tax-exempt bonds is less than 2 percent of the adjusted basis of the total portfolio. Consult a qualified tax advisor for specific guidance in your personal situation if you are unclear about whether interest expense of a loan is disallowed as a deduction or not.

Reporting Tax-Exempt Income

Even though income from municipals is tax-exempt from federal income tax, it still must be reported. Unless you are subject to the Alternative Minimum Tax, the amount you report will not have any bearing on your tax liability and is reported for information purposes only.

Social Security Considerations

Income from tax-exempt bonds may reduce the amount of the benefits you are receiving from Social Security. The complex formula looks at how much you are receiving from Social Security, your adjusted gross income, and interest from tax-exempt bonds. The calculation arrives at a potentially greater tax liability, depending on several factors including the amount of tax-exempt interest income you carry.

This potential reduction should be examined before plunging into an aggressive program of buying tax-exempt bonds, as it may significantly reduce your Social Security benefits. This would have the effect of reducing your overall return on retirement assets and almost certainly not be worth the risk of losing benefits.

State Tax Treatment

Most states exempt from income tax interest earned on municipal bonds issued within the state. Of course, this doesn't apply to those states that don't have an income tax. This general rule is not universal. A handful of states tax income from at least some of the tax-exempt bonds issued within the state. If the state where you live taxes interest from bonds issued within its borders, you do not have access to one of the advantages of owning municipal bonds. Federal income tax rates are much higher than state rates; however, every exemption helps.

Municipal bonds' main attraction to investors is the tax exemption on interest income. When you can get that exemption on both federal and state income taxes, it makes those bonds more attractive than bonds where only the federal exemption is available. Mutual funds that specialize in "triple exempt" bonds, meaning the bonds are not subject to federal, state, or local taxes, are sold in states with high income tax rates. The funds buy bonds issued in those states to take advantage of the tax exemptions. For more information on these funds, see Chapter 9.

> **Red Flag**
>
> Some states tax bonds issued within their borders as well as those issued outside their borders, although they may exempt interest from income taxes on certain types of bonds. Your financial professional can tell you what the status of bond taxation is in your state and how it relates to any bonds you are considering.

Market Discount Tax Issues

Certain market conditions will cause the market value of a bond to drop below its face value. These include a change in interest rates or a negative change in the issuer's credit rating. If an investor buys a discounted bond and later sells the bond for more than she paid for it or holds it to maturity and redeems it for full face value, a taxable situation exists.

For example, if interest rates rise, the value of an existing bond will drop in the secondary market. An investor may buy a $5,000 bond for $4,200. If the investor holds the bond to maturity and redeems it for the face value of $5,000, the $800 difference is considered ordinary income. If the bond is sold before maturity, there is a formula for calculating how much gain is attributed to ordinary income. Your tax professional can calculate this for you.

The earlier discussion of original issue discount did not create ordinary income tax liability because that discount was an issuer decision. It is only when market forces discount the value of a bond that it creates an ordinary income tax situation.

Taxable Municipal Bonds

Although we think of municipal bonds as being tax-exempt—at least from federal income tax—there are bonds sold that are subject to tax. These bonds are taxable because the IRS deems them issued for some private purpose and not for the public good. A prime example would be municipal bonds to build a sports stadium or entertainment venue. The income from these bonds is generally subject to federal income tax and usually state and local taxes, too. The yields may be comparable to similar corporate bonds.

Insured Municipal Bonds

Although municipal bonds, as a group, have a better safety record than corporate bonds, many investors still want more protection from the possibility of default. These investors turn to insured bonds for the assurance they need.

Extra Protection of Insurance

Some bond investors—in fact, it may be true of most—are very concerned about preserving their capital invested in the securities. This is one of the reasons investors will pick U.S. Treasury notes and bonds, which usually pay the least but are the safest. Other investors are more willing to step out on the risk scale in return for a higher reward.

One of the ways an issuer can make its bonds more attractive to investors is to have them insured. There are several reasons an issuer might decide to go to the expense of insurance, but the bottom line is that insurance enhances the bonds in the eyes of investors. This makes issuing bonds easier.

> **Market Place**
>
> The municipal bond market is crowded with some 50,000-plus issues. Some issuers have to enhance their bonds to make them more attractive to investors. Bond insurance is the primary way to attract investors because it guarantees the timely payment of interest and principal.

Bond Insurance Companies

Bond insurance guarantees investors will receive interest payments and principal in a timely manner. If a bond issuer finds itself unable to make the required payments, the insurance company will step in and make the payments.

The companies that insure municipal bonds are of the highest quality in their own creditworthiness, earning AAA ratings from the major rating agencies. These insurance companies only insure bonds, so they aren't at risk from losses in other types of coverage. States closely regulate the insurance companies, since these insurers must step in if a municipality falters in its ability to pay interest or principal in a timely manner.

Insured bonds lower the cost to the issuer because they are lower risks to the investor. Close to one half of all newly issued municipal bonds are insured, which reflects investor demand for more secure products. This is consistent with the general conservative nature of bonds.

Benefits of Insured Bonds

Is it necessary that all bonds you consider for investment be insured? Probably not, unless you are more comfortable with the security the insurance brings. Bonds from municipalities that are financially secure and that are tied to solid projects or assets may not need the extra protection. However, this is a personal preference call. You will need to decide where your comfort zone is with risk in bond investing.

Buying insured bonds does offer some benefits that you might want to consider. These include:

Security—Obviously, this is the primary reason for investing in insured bonds. If the issuer cannot meet timely interest or principal payments, the insurance company will step in and make you whole. Without this insurance, you may or may not get your money eventually.

Creditworthiness—Municipal bonds insured by AAA-rated insurance companies are assigned their credit rating: AAA. This puts them on par with any bond on the market.

Liquidity—The secondary market for municipal bonds is a hit-or-miss proposition. If you own a well-known, frequently traded bond, you may be able to sell quickly at a reasonable price. However, if your bond is less well known and traded less frequently, you may be forced to discount your bond to sell it in the secondary market. Insured bonds are a different story. The secondary market is full of actively traded insured bonds. Investors know they are buying a safe bond, which eases the way to quicker transactions.

Yield—You can usually earn a slightly higher yield with a Triple-A-rated insured bond than with regular Triple-A-rated bonds. The market judges bonds that have earned AAA credit rating without insurance as stronger than insured bonds, so the yields are slightly lower than insured bonds.

Revenue bonds—Some investors shy away from revenue bonds, which tend to be more risky than general obligation bonds because repayment is tied to some specific project rather than the taxing authority of the municipality. Insured revenue bonds can take that concern away. Revenue bonds and certain other types of municipal bonds that are not general obligation bonds can be enhanced by insurance that removes much of the perceived risk. These bonds often pay a higher yield than general obligation bonds.

Scrutiny—Investors can take some comfort in knowing that before an insurance company agrees to insure a bond issue, it will thoroughly inspect and analyze the issuer and the issue. This scrutiny is detailed and complex and it assures investors that professionals have examined the issue and found it sound. Like most insurance policies, the sick can't buy one.

Market Place

The benefits of insurance are so dramatic that many issuers apply for the coverage, but not all are accepted. The insurance companies are very careful about which issuers they will insure and shoot for a no-losses record.

What Bond Insurance Can and Can't Do

If a municipality finds itself in a hard situation because of difficult economic circumstances, for example, and it can't make interest or principal payments, the insurance will make the payments. This safety net keeps the value of insured municipal bonds high in difficult economic times when compared to uninsured bonds.

However, insurance does not specifically protect the market value of municipal bonds in the secondary market. Changes in interest rates in particular can have a negative affect on bond values. If you have to sell your bond before maturity, you may incur a loss—that is, you may have to sell your bond for less than face value. Bond insurance won't help you here. The loss in value was a result of your decision to sell before maturity, not any fault of the issuer.

The Least You Need to Know

- Municipal bonds are issued by state and local government organizations to fund civic improvement projects such as roads and other capital improvements.

- Interest income from municipal bonds is exempt from federal income taxes and may be exempt from state and local taxes in the state where issued.

- There are several other tax issues such as capital gains and losses, AMT, and other situations that may create tax liabilities.

- AAA-rated insurance companies guarantee municipal bond issuers will pay interest income and principal in a timely manner.

Chapter 8

Calculating Bond Values

In This Chapter

- Factors that influence bond prices
- Types of yields
- Links between maturities and yields
- Calculating bond values

What is the price of a share of IBM stock? That's an easy question to answer—there are hundreds of sites on the Internet to find that information, or you can call your stockbroker. If you are a long-term investor or a day-trader, the answer is the same. However, if you are a bond investor, determining what a bond is worth may not be that simple or easy. Depending on your investment objectives, you may not care what the current market price is. The approach to valuing bonds depends on your investment objective to a certain extent, and the type of bonds you buy. The factors that influence bond values and how bonds react to those factors may seem confusing at first, but do make sense.

What Moves the Bond Market

The bond market keeps a close watch on indicators that show how fast or slow the economy is growing, with an ultimate eye on how those factors will influence interest rates. A change in the rate of inflation may be revealed by this same group of indicators.

The Fed Is Watching

The Federal Reserve Board through its Open Market Committee closely monitors a broad range of economic indicators of the economy's health. They are primarily concerned with seeing that the economy grows at a manageable pace and that inflation stays in check. An economy that grows too fast will cause inflation, which can be devastating if it gets out of control. The Fed, as it is known, can cool the economy by raising interest rates, which makes it more expensive for businesses and consumers to borrow money. If the economy slows too much, the Fed can lower interest rates, which encourages borrowing, business expansion, and consumer spending.

Market Place

While politicians can play a role in the economy, it is too dynamic for a central government to control. The evidence of this is that sometimes the economy is rotten and no politician ever steps forward to claim credit.

What everyone (investors, businesses, and consumers) wants is the "Goldilocks" economy—not too hot and not too cold, but just right. The economy was in that sweet spot in the 1990s, especially the last half of that decade, which witnessed the strongest bull stock market in history. Unfortunately, the economy is too dynamic to stay in one configuration for very long. It was already coming unraveled when the tragedy of September 11, 2001, struck. The next few years saw the stock market give up most of the gains of the bull market (the NASDAQ Composite Index lost one half of its value). The economy slipped into a recession, which is defined as a decline in the Gross National Product for two quarters in a row.

The Fed (the Open Market Committee meets eight times a year) responded with 16 straight interest rate cuts, dropping their key interest rate down to a record 1 percent. That stimulation got the economy moving again, but as it did, the Fed began to worry that it was expanding too fast and began raising interest rates to keep inflationary pressures under control. The strategy worked, but rising interest rates, as we'll see next, are trouble for bond investors.

Importance of Economic Indicators

Key economic indicators give clues about which direction the economy is headed, which in turn tell you something about how this change may affect interest rates. Indicators that report recently acquired data are more important than those that are delayed for months. For example, unemployment numbers come out monthly and are important indicators of the economy's health. Strong growth in the number of people employed may show the economy is expanding rapidly, which could lead to inflation.

Retail sales are another important indicator because so much of our national economic engine is driven by consumer spending. If consumer spending is way up, that could create inflationary pressures.

You don't have to be an economist to follow these indicators. There are a number of websites listed in Appendix B that provide excellent information and commentary on the economy and what it means to bond investors.

> **Bond Tip**
>
> Investing in bonds is like investing in stocks: if you are a buy-and-hold investor, don't pay much attention to the talking heads on cable talk shows who worry about every day in the market like it was the pivotal moment in investing history. It isn't.

What's So Bad About Inflation?

Inflation is a concern for almost every type of investor because it destroys value, especially the future value of your investments. Although some assets such as real estate and gold may appreciate during periods of inflation, many other investments suffer because they do not appreciate as fast as inflation, especially fixed-rate instruments such as bonds. Inflation means the price of goods and services will cost more in the future than they cost today. We've come to expect rising prices over time and a small amount of inflation is not a serious problem—people's incomes can adjust.

However, when inflation rises at a rapid pace, incomes don't keep pace and investments can't grow as fast. The future value of investments that can't grow as fast as inflation is compromised. You can easily see the problem for bond investors. Bonds, for the most part, pay a fixed rate. When bonds are issued there is some inflation growth built into the bond's interest rate. However, if inflation grows at a faster pace than anticipated, then the bond's interest income is worth less and the face value at redemption is worth less.

Inflation is like a silent tax that destroys value, and that is why the Fed is so aggressive in keeping it under control. For bond investors, the cure can sometimes be as bad as the disease. As the Fed raises interest rates, existing bonds are negatively affected as we'll see.

Bond Values and Investment Objectives

Your investment objectives have much more influence on the importance of the current market value of your bond than for just about any other security or investment. However, there are no absolutes and you can never be sure your objectives won't change thanks to circumstances you did not foresee.

The Two Major Investment Objectives

Investors who own bonds usually do so with one of two objectives in mind. The first objective is to buy and hold a bond until its maturity. This is the most popular investment objective with investors who own bonds. The second investment objective is to trade bonds on the secondary market in hopes of earning higher interest rates and trading for a profit.

> **Bond Tip**
>
> Most investors buy individual bonds for their steady income and safety of principal. They hold the bonds until maturity and reinvest the face value. Don't be lured into trading in the secondary market by the promise of high returns—there are no promises in trading, only expenses.

Buy-and-Hold Investors

If you are a buy-and-hold investor, the current market value of your bond doesn't mean much to you. You bought the bond with the idea that you would hold it to maturity, collecting the semi-annual interest payments along the way. Interest rates can change and your bond can fluctuate in value on the secondary market, but it doesn't affect your objective because you will collect the full face value at maturity regardless of the market value (more about this in the following sections).

The Bond Trader

The bond trader is looking for a better interest rate or to sell for a profit as interest rates change. This investor is concerned about monetary policy, interest rates, inflation, and other factors that affect bond prices. Bond traders may hold their bonds for a long or short period before trading, depending on their trading philosophy. Because of the transaction costs, bond traders must make significant gains on each trade to remain profitable. For many of the reasons cited in Chapter 4, trading bonds as an investment strategy is not for beginners. You need a thorough understanding of the market and how it works to improve your chances for success.

Is There a Middle Ground?

You don't have to choose between one absolute or the other. Some buy-and-hold investors find it makes sense to stay on top of the market to pick opportunities to buy or sell when conditions seem right. Likewise, a person who mainly trades bonds may find a good situation where holding on to a bond rather than trading is the best choice.

Interest Rates and Bond Yields

Most bonds have a fixed interest rate, also called a stated interest rate or nominal yield. Current yield is the rate of return the bond earns at the current market value of the bond. When market interest rates change, the market value of a bond changes and so does its current yield. This opens the door to potentially confusing terms investors hear about bond yields.

> **Red Flag**
>
> It is very important that you grasp the differences in yields that may be quoted for bonds. Knowing what they mean will save you from making a poor investment decision.

Different Types of Bond Yields

Bond investors will hear and read about bond yields in several different contexts. The term "yield" can mean several different values depending on the context. How and when those terms apply is important to your understanding of bonds.

The basic definition of yield is the current yield. This yield is an expression of the interest income as a percentage of the current market value of the bond. The current yield only tells you at what rate you are earning interest on your bond based on the market value of the bond at that particular

moment. It doesn't tell you anything about what
the bond will yield over the life of the bond if
you held it to maturity. That calculation is called
"yield-to-maturity." It is more complicated than
the current yield because it looks at the bond's
capacity to produce income over the life of the
bond. We'll discuss yield-to-maturity in a separate
section in this chapter.

Understanding a Bond's Current Yield

A bond's current yield isn't particularly helpful
except when you are looking at how bond values
react to changes in market interest rates. If interest
rates stay the same, the current yield stays the
same. For example, if you buy a bond at issue for
$1,000 and it pays $60 per year in interest, the
stated interest rate is 6 percent. The current yield
is 6 percent ($60 ÷ $1,000 = .06) also. In this case,
the stated interest rate (6 percent) and the yield (6
percent) are the same. However, if interest rates
change, so will the current yield.

New bonds issued at new interest rates will have
a different yield. Existing bond yields must be
adjusted to match new market yields so the bonds
can trade in the secondary market. This adjustment
means the value of some bonds will rise, while the
value of other bonds will fall, depending on their
fixed interest payment. For example, if you had a
$1,000 five-year bond that paid a stated interest
rate of 6 percent, the current yield would be 6 percent (the previous example). If new bonds are issued
with a stated interest rate of 7 percent for the same

maturity as remains on your bond, what does that do to the value of your bond? Clearly, an investor would choose the 7 percent bond over your 6 percent bond, all other factors being roughly equal. If you are going to sell your bond, you must adjust its value so the current yield will equal that of the new bond. This would mean an investor could buy your bond at a discount and still earn the same return (7 percent) that the new bonds were paying.

The current yield of your bond must rise to 7 percent, matching the new rate. This is done by reducing the value of your bond. Your bond must yield the same as other bonds on the market or it will not sell. Since the interest income ($60 per year) is fixed, the only way to increase the yield (which is the rate of return that $60 represents) is to discount the price of the bond.

Market Place

Understanding the current yield and how bond prices must adjust can be confusing, but keep in mind that for bonds to sell in the secondary market, they must match the current yield available from other bonds. That means the bond price is adjusted up or down so the yield equals the current market rate.

The discount is calculated by looking at the future value of interest payments over the number of years remaining to maturity. The easiest way to do this is to use an online calculator such as The Hedgehog's Calculators (www.hedge-hog.com). This interactive calculator lets you enter current information about a bond and new interest rates to see what happens to the bond's value.

This formula works the other way also. If market interest rates fall, your bond will be worth more—that is, it will sell at a premium because its fixed rate of interest is higher than the rate for newly issued bonds. For example, if new bond yields dropped to 5 percent, what would your bond be worth? Your premium will depend on years left to maturity (or call—see the next section). In actual trading on the secondary market, other factors such as supply and demand, maturities, and so on would have an affect on bond prices, but the major change in bond values would be driven by changes in interest rates.

This points out why interest rates are so important to bond holders. We noted earlier that there are certain bonds that adjust for inflation and such, but for most bonds holding them to maturity does not change the face value.

For fixed-income bonds, the rule on interest rates, yields, and bond values is:

- As interest rates go up, bond values go down, and yields go up
- As interest rates go down, bond values go up, and yields go down

It is important to note that if you plan to hold your bond to maturity, none of this matters—your bond is still worth $1,000 when you redeem it no matter what interest rates have done.

Maturity and Interest Rates

While changes in interest rates affect all fixed-income bonds, they don't affect them the same. As discussed previously in Chapter 3, the longer the maturity, the greater the risk that something negative will happen to interest rates (or other factors, too). This is why long-term bonds pay a higher rate than short-term bonds. You are compensated for the additional risk of holding the bond for a longer period.

That's the way it is supposed to work. The relationship of short- and long-term interest rates is called the *yield curve*. If you plotted a normal yield curve on a graph, you would see a chart that climbs fairly sharply between short and intermediate rates but the angle of ascent is not so great between intermediate rates and long-term rates. When the yield curve looks different than this, it may mean an opportunity or change is at hand.

def•i•ni•tion

The **yield curve** is the plotting of short-, intermediate-, and long-term interest rates to observe the relationship. U.S. Treasury issues are often used since they have no credit risk to distort the interest rates.

A sharp curve suggests a large difference between short- and long-term rates that may mean an opportunity exists for investors to move some of their assets into longer-term bonds. If the yield curve isn't a curve at all, but fairly flat, there is little or no premium for investing in long-term bonds. Given that there is more risk in long-term bonds, most investors would choose to avoid them when there was no premium in the interest rate. When short-term interest rates are higher than long-term rates, the yield curve is inverted. This usually signals that the market anticipates rates falling and it is not a good time to be investing in long-term bonds. An inverted yield curve is also considered by some as a signal of an approaching recession.

Summing Up Current Yield

Current yield is helpful in determining what a bond is returning based on its current market value. It is also helpful in determining how much of a discount or premium a bond will sell at in a changing interest rate environment.

We can approximate the market value of bonds when interest rates change using the current yield formula. In Chapter 3, we discussed the risks of interest rate change. A table in that chapter showed how the market value of a bond changed under different market interest rates. Here is that table again. The original bond has a face value of $1,000 and a 6 percent coupon.

| Maturity | Interest Rates | | | | |
	4%	5%	6%	7%	8%
1 year	$1,019	$1,010	$1,000	$991	$981
3 years	$1,056	$1,027	$1,000	$974	$948
5 years	$1,089	$1,043	$1,000	$959	$920
10 years	$1,162	$1,077	$1,000	$930	$866
30 years	$1,346	$1,154	$1,000	$876	$775

It is important to note that the more years to maturity, the more dramatically interest rate changes affected bond values. Notice the difference between a 5 percent bond with 1 year left to maturity and a 5 percent bond with 30 years left. This is confirmation of the risk of long-term bonds and why you should expect a premium in interest rates for holding them.

Bond Tip

Investors looking for the balance between high yields and lower risk often look to the intermediate-term bonds (7 to 10 years) where there is some premium for a longer term, but less price risk than true long-term bonds.

Duration

Duration is another measurement that lets you compare the price risk of bonds with different maturities, call dates, and coupon rates. It is a very complicated measurement that has several variations, but in its simplest form measures in years how long it will take the bond to repay the price of the bond through interest payments. Variations on duration measure price sensitivity and how much a bond's value will change based on changing market interest rates. Some simple conclusions from studying duration are that bonds with high coupon rates are less sensitive to interest rate changes (because they return more of the face value quicker) than bonds with low coupon rates.

Bond mutual fund managers use the variety of duration calculations to help construct portfolios that match their needs and risk tolerances. Individual investors with substantial assets in individual bonds should rely on a trusted financial advisor for information on duration as it relates to your total portfolio.

Yield-to-Maturity

The most important "yield" number you need to know is yield-to-maturity (YTM). This calculation gives you a much clearer picture of what you will earn over the life of a bond than the current yield. However, it is a very complicated calculation and most people rely on their stockbrokers or online calculators for the number.

YTM Is Your Best Valuation

Most of the time, when you hear bond yields quoted in the news media, you are hearing YTM, since this number is a more accurate reflection of what a bond is truly worth.

YTM is defined as the annual yield of a bond assuming it is held to maturity, considering the current market value, stated interest rate, reinvestment of interest payments at the current market rate, number of years to maturity, and any discount or premium paid for the bond. It is a complex calculation that is not easy to solve without the help of a sophisticated calculator or computer software. You can find online calculators such as Money-Chimp (www.moneychimp.com) under the calculators section. The YTM is an important number because is gives you a much more accurate picture of what a bond is worth under the best trading conditions and with a disciplined investor (if you don't reinvest the interest payments, your yield drops dramatically).

> **Bond Tip**
>
> Yield-to-maturity calculations can be used for any maturity you choose as long as it doesn't exceed the bond's actual maturity. For example, if you have a 10-year bond, you can calculate the YTM for any date before the real maturity if you plan to sell at a specific time or to check "what if" scenarios.

Yield-to-Call or Yield-to-Worst

The YTM calculation assumes you hold the bond until maturity. However, from previous discussions we know that a number of bonds have call features that allow the issuer to force redemption earlier. When that is the case, you are prudent to insist that your broker quote you the yield-to-call or yield-to-worst number. This number assumes your bond will be called at the earliest possible date on the indenture. You don't know when it will be called, but you must assume it will be called at the earliest possible moment.

This is important because it dramatically changes what your YTM numbers for a bond look like. Consider a $1,000 10-year bond with a 7 percent coupon that can be called after three years. Interest rates have fallen and you are offered the bond at the one year mark. The market price of the bond is $1,050. If you calculate the YTM at nine years, it comes out to 6.26 percent. However, since rates have fallen, the bond may be called in two years. The yield-to-call is only 4.37 percent. There is almost two full percentage points difference in the calculations. If your stockbroker quotes you 6.26 percent as the YTM, you might think this was a good deal. However, the yield-to-call (the more likely result), tells a different story. This is also the yield-to-worst. Some bonds have multiple call dates. You should use the lowest (soonest) date as the yield-to-worst for a more conservative and realistic idea of when you might lose the bond to a call.

The Least You Need to Know

- The bond market is very sensitive to economic indicators that measure inflation and interest rates.

- Current yield measures the return you are earning on your bond based on its current market value.

- Bonds with longer maturities are more vulnerable to interest rate risk and price changes.

- Yield-to-maturity is the most accurate way to value a bond, with yield-to-call being the conservative step for callable bonds.

Chapter 9

Bond Mutual Funds

In This Chapter

- Differences from individual bonds
- Benefits/drawbacks of bond funds
- Types of bond funds
- Exchange-traded funds and other investments

Investors can buy bonds as individual securities or as packages in mutual funds, exchange-traded funds, unit investment trusts, and other securities. There are many benefits to buying your bonds in a mutual fund (the most popular choice of all the package options). You have many reasons to choose mutual funds, not the least of which is convenience—and that's an important factor. However, with all the benefits of investing in bond mutual funds come some costs, literally. You will pay for the privilege of using mutual funds or one of the other packages of bond investments. What is more, these packages do not provide the same type of investment return as individual bonds do. Investors have choices to make, and that's a good thing, but be sure you know what the alternatives are before you put down your money.

A Bond Is a Bond

An individual bond, regardless of the type, has certain characteristics that make it a popular investment. These attributes set it apart from stocks and other investments, which is one of the main reasons you should have some in your portfolio.

Review of Bond Attributes

Most bonds pay a fixed interest rate over a specified period, dividing the payments into semiannual installments. At the end of this period, the company issuing the bond redeems it for the full face value. Investors like bonds for their steady income and safety of principal (with highly rated issues). Investment-grade bonds of moderate maturity do not correlate with stocks, meaning many of the factors that move stocks in one direction may have the opposite or no effect on bonds.

Individual bonds can be bought at issue or in the secondary market, although the market for specific securities may or may not be liquid. Changes in interest rates can have a dramatic effect on the market price and yield of individual bonds.

> **Bond Tip** _____
>
> Individual bonds are valued for steady income and predictable return of principal when the bond matures. Mutual funds that invest in bonds can't offer this same assurance because they have no maturity and your income depends on how well the manager picks bonds and what the fund's objectives are.

How Mutual Funds Are Different

Mutual funds are pools of investor dollars managed by professionals with certain investment objectives and often targeting a specific type of bond, whether it is by issue, issuer, maturity, or some combination.

Attributes of Mutual Funds

Mutual funds benefit from professional management and, where it makes sense, diversification across numerous issues. Bond funds may be taxable or nontaxable and come in a variety of maturities. Income and capital gains (and losses) are generally passed to investors. You can buy mutual funds directly from the fund company at no markup. Some mutual funds do have loads (fees), which are deducted from your investment, and most have a management fee of some type.

Individual bonds have a maturity. Bond mutual funds do not. This can be a benefit or a problem, depending on how market interest rates go and how the fund manager has positioned the fund (more about this next).

Benefits/Drawbacks of Bond Mutual Funds

Bond mutual funds are a popular choice for many investors looking to diversify their portfolio, but unwilling to buy individual bonds. There are many benefits to investing in bond mutual funds; however, there are some drawbacks that can be problematic.

Benefits of Bond Mutual Funds

Bond mutual funds share many of the generic benefits that apply to all mutual funds:

Professional management—Bonds are, in many ways, more complicated than stocks because there is less information available on individual issues including pricing and so on. Professional management in selecting issues is a real plus.

Diversification—Diversification issues in bond investing are different than those for stocks. For example, if you only invest in U.S. Treasury issues, there is no need to diversify for credit risk, because there is no credit risk. If you buy 1 10-year T-note or 100 10-year T-notes, you haven't changed your credit risk profile. Diversification is more important when you begin looking at high-yield corporate bonds. These more risky investments will benefit from diversification and a professional bond mutual fund can provide not only the diversification, but the quantity of issues to make diversification work.

Bond Tip

Professional management is a value added by bond mutual funds. Bonds can be difficult to understand because information on individual issues can be hard to find and pricing is not readily available.

Inexpensive—If you stick with a no-load fund and buy direct, your transaction costs are very low or zero to buy into a bond mutual fund (or redeem shares for that matter). With individual bonds, you pay commissions and markups both ways on the buy and sell, which will reduce your profit or increase your loss. The bond mutual fund will let you *dollar cost average*, which is an effective way to build a position over time. When you buy individual bonds, you pay a premium because the market is geared to large transactions (in the hundreds of thousands of dollars). Mutual funds make those buys of this size and can get the best prices.

def•i•ni•tion

Dollar cost averaging is an investment strategy that says you should invest the same amount on a regular basis to achieve the best average price. For example, if you invest $25 every two weeks in a bond mutual fund you can buy shares at the current price. If share prices are up, you buy fewer shares and if share prices are down, you buy more shares. Over time, your average price is lower than if you tried to time the market with buys.

Price transparency—Unlike individual bonds for which the true cost may be obscured by broker markups and commissions, bond funds offer transparency in pricing. Mutual funds are quoted for buying or selling at their net asset value or NAV. This is the sum of the fund's assets (holdings) less its debts divided by outstanding shares. Funds recalculate their NAV at the close of the market each business day. You can find prices in many large newspapers or on many websites, including the website of the fund management company. If you buy directly from the investment company (and you usually should), you don't pay any commissions, markups, or other transaction costs.

Convenience and liquidity—Bond mutual funds are simply more convenient than buying individual bonds. There is much less to keep up with, even if you have a stockbroker working for you. You can set up an account for a minimum amount (often $1,000, compared to $5,000 minimum for a single bond). Bond mutual funds are highly liquid. If you need all or some of your money, you can usually get it within a business day or so. Selling an individual bond may go swiftly or not depending on the market for that particular issue.

Bond Tip

Liquidity of bond mutual funds should not be underestimated. The difficulty of selling an individual bond before you anticipated the need can mean giving a big discount on the price. With a bond mutual fund, you know exactly what you will get and when you can get it.

Automatic reinvestment—With bond mutual funds you can have any income automatically reinvested in the fund. If you don't need the income for living expenses, this is a great way to build your account balance and if you hold the fund in a tax-deferred retirement account, you won't have to pay taxes on any gains from taxable transactions. With individual bonds, you must find a new investment for your interest checks twice a year.

Drawbacks of Bond Mutual Funds

Bond mutual funds are not the perfect investment. They have some issues that must be addressed:

Expenses—Bond mutual funds can be very expensive investments if you are not careful. Some funds carry heavy expense loads that take a large bite out of your investment and consume ongoing management fees. There are ways to avoid these funds, such as investing in inexpensive no-load funds and index funds. However, even these funds have ongoing expenses (more on expenses later).

Taxes—If you invest in a taxable bond fund (and it will be unless it specifically states otherwise), you may get hit with hefty capital gains distributions if the fund manager is constantly buying and selling bonds to meet investment objectives. It may be wise to hold a taxable bond fund in a tax-deferred retirement account, but check with your tax advisor for specific information about your situation.

Red Flag

The fund manager for a bond mutual fund may have a different priority than you do. He is interested in keeping the fund's share value high, while you may be more interested in a steady income. This can be a problem if you are counting on this income for living expenses.

ATM—Some municipal bonds as mentioned in Chapter 7 fall under the umbrella of the Alternative Minimum Tax. You may be forced to count income on your federal taxes that would be otherwise exempt. Bond mutual funds that invest in municipal bonds that are captured under ATM must declare so to investors. If you are subject to ATM and hold shares of a mutual fund that invests in these types of municipal bonds, you must calculate how much income they represent to the total fund and declare that on your income tax. It can get complicated.

Interest rate changes—Many investors buy bonds for the predictable income stream they provide and are not concerned about the market value so much. However, fund managers can't afford such an attitude because declining bond prices (as interest rates rise) mean the shares of the mutual funds decline in value. The fund manager may be forced to reshuffle the fund's holdings, which could affect the income you were expecting.

Uncertain income—When you buy an individual bond, you know what to expect (and when) in interest payments for most bonds. You can plan on the fixed income and plan on the face amount being returned at maturity. With bond mutual funds you do not know what your income will be because fund managers are buying and selling bonds in response to market conditions. Mutual funds pay dividends monthly or quarterly, but you can't know what to expect. The exception might be bond index funds that buy and hold a portfolio of bonds that matches one of the bond indexes. Index funds tend to be stable with little turnover, so you may find that their income is more predictable.

Mutual Fund Expenses

All mutual funds (stocks as well as bonds) have expenses that come out of your invested dollars and profits or losses. Some funds charge very high fees for the value they believe is added, while other funds charge very low fees. Over time, guess which type of fund returns the most to investors?

Sold or Bought

Some mutual funds are only sold by brokers or other financial professionals—you can't buy directly from the fund management company. These funds are called loaded funds and should be avoided. You will pay a large percentage of your investment dollars in sales commissions, which reduces your chances of making a profit in the fund (you first have to earn enough to repay the lost dollars paid in commissions).

Other funds called no-load funds allow you to buy directly from the investment company and avoid paying any sales or commission charges—all of your money is invested in the fund. This is your best bet because you start off even and not in the hole as you do with loaded funds.

Active vs. Passive Management

Mutual funds are either actively or passively managed. As you might guess, those terms describe the amount of activity the fund manager generates in an effort to provide superior results to investors.

The amount of activity can also be related to the fees and expenses connected to the fund.

> **Bond Tip**
>
> Buy no-load bond mutual funds. These funds don't charge a sales fee, which comes out of your investing dollars. There are too many good no-load options to pay a sales fee that adds nothing to the quality of the fund, only to the quality of life for the broker.

Actively Managed Funds

An actively managed bond fund, for example, will trade bonds in and out of its account frequently in a strategy to beat "the market" in results for the fund. "The market" in this case is usually one of the bond indexes such as the Lehman Brothers 10-Year Municipal Bond Index. There is little evidence that actively managing bond funds (or stock funds) adds any real value and it most certainly contributes to the drag on profits. Fund managers may be successful for short periods, but seldom sustain their winning streak, because the market usually will not stay in one place long enough for a single investment strategy to be successful year after year. More importantly, simply because a fund manager has been successful in the past is not a predictor of any future success. The number of fund managers who consistently do better than the market is very small when you consider the thousands of mutual funds that must be managed.

Passively Managed Funds

Passively managed funds include those that track certain indexes and others that follow a buy-and-don't-trade-often philosophy. Index funds are the ultimate in passive funds. They track a particular bond index by matching the holdings of the index. If the index does well, so does the fund and if the index does not do well, then neither does the fund. Index funds don't employ managers in the same way actively managed funds do. Their goal is to match the index and avoid other expenses that may detract from the hoped-for earnings. The fund does not buy or sell any assets unless the index it tracks does, so the fund has very low operating costs.

One predictor of investment success is expense: the lower your expense of investing (fees, commissions, and so on), the higher your chances of coming out ahead. Index bond mutual funds are the best vehicle for this type of investing. However, you can also find bond mutual funds that have an investing philosophy that is more "buy-and-hold" than active trading. These funds focus on income and don't turn over their portfolio as often as other actively traded funds.

Bond Tip

Some experts will agree that expenses are the single most important determinant in predicting long-term investment success of most mutual bond funds. The math is simple: funds that have heavy expenses must earn that much more just to break even.

Types of Mutual Funds: Investors' Choices

There are over 4,200 bond mutual funds on the market, so you may be wondering, "Where do I start?" The first step is to figure out your investment objectives and determine what types of bonds you want in your portfolio.

Investors have a wide range of choices when it comes to picking bond mutual funds. Do you want a taxable or tax-free fund, or both? What credit rating do you want, and what about maturity? All of these criteria go into finding the right mutual bond fund to fit your needs.

You saw earlier that bond mutual funds can provide diversification, which is important for minimizing risks with some bonds. Mutual funds can also provide you with access to a variety of maturities in one portfolio, which is also an important way to protect against changes in interest rates. In Chapter 10, I'll talk more about building a portfolio using individual bonds and mutual funds, but now let's focus on the different types of bond mutual funds that you might use in your portfolio. These definitions are broad and not always followed by every mutual fund. In addition, there are many bond mutual funds that attempt to carve out their own niche by being slightly different than close competitors.

U.S. Government Funds

These bond funds invest at least 80 percent of their assets in U.S. Treasury securities and U.S. agency bonds. The funds may also use options, futures, and interest rate swaps to achieve goals of high returns.

General U.S. Government Bond Funds

Bond funds that invest in securities that are backed or substantially backed by the U.S. government, such as agency issues, make up 80 percent of the portfolio. Many of these funds carry a mixed maturity of issues.

Short-Term U.S. Government Bond Funds

Short-term U.S. government bond funds keep their maturities under five years and in many cases around three years, but this will vary with each fund. Normally, these funds stick with U.S. Treasury and agency issues, but read the description carefully, because some funds allow a small percentage of the portfolio to be invested in corporate bonds.

Intermediate U.S. Government Bond Funds

These popular funds focus on U.S. issues in the 5- to 10-year maturity range, although some may go as low as three-year maturity. Many of the bonds concentrate their investments in U.S. issues up to 80 percent of the total portfolio, but may fill the remainder with a variety of derivatives and other bonds.

> **Bond Tip**
>
> Intermediate government bonds, specifically the 10-year U.S. Treasury note, is the gold standard for safety when measuring other securities. Bond funds that focus on T-notes in the 10 year and lower range are very popular because this is where you get a kick for interest rate risk, but have a chance to retreat if needed.

Long-Term U.S. Government Bond Funds

Long-term U.S. government funds are all over the board when it comes to investment policy and maturity. Pay careful attention to the investment strategy and what other securities the fund holds. Some long-term bond funds hold zero-coupon bonds (more about those in Chapter 10). These funds are self-liquidating, meaning on a certain date the bonds mature and the fund pays out its assets and is closed. Long-term bonds, as we have learned, carry the most risk and should bring you the highest return. Compare the returns of long-term bond funds to shorter-term funds to see if the risk is being rewarded with a higher return.

Corporate Bond Funds

Corporate bond funds provide the investor with the best protection through diversification of all bond types. Corporate bonds carry the most risk and the investor benefits the most from professional management of the corporate bond fund portfolio.

Short-Term Corporate Bond Funds

Short-term corporate bond funds invest between two thirds and 80 percent of their assets in corporate bonds with maturities of less than five years. Some funds limit maturities to closer to three years. Read the fund profile carefully as many short-term corporate bond funds also invest in options, futures, and other speculative securities. Short-term bond funds should be the more conservative of the corporate fund class, because the overall exposure is for shorter maturities; however, this means returns will be lower.

Intermediate Corporate Bond Funds

Intermediate corporate bond funds may stretch out maturities to 10 years, although many will come in under the 10-year mark. For this extra exposure to interest rate risk, you should expect a premium in return over short-term corporate bond funds and certainly a higher return than the U.S. Treasury intermediate funds. However, with this hoped-for increased return comes extra risk and potential for losses.

Long-Term Corporate Bond Funds

Long-term bond funds usually state an investment goal of maximum return or something along those lines. While they may invest mainly in corporate bonds, most do not limit themselves to that strict category and may also invest in foreign bonds and other securities. When a fund targets maximum return, you can expect an aggressive approach, which can lead to significant gains if the fund manager is on target and big disappointments if she is wrong.

High-Yield Corporate Bond Funds

The only bond funds that may be more aggressive than long-term corporate bonds are high-yield bond funds. High-yield corporate bonds are another term for junk bonds. These are bonds with low credit ratings issued by companies on shaky financial ground. Funds may temper the risks of investing in credit-poor companies by spreading investments over a range of industries so to diversify by sector. However, there is no getting around the high-risk nature of these investments. High-yield funds should live up to their name—that is, you should expect high dividends (income) or you are taking too much risk for too little reward. A premium of 2 percent is not unusual.

Bond Tip

High-yield corporate bonds are very risky for the average investor to buy individually. Professional management of bond funds can be worth a great deal in discerning the better buys in this market.

Municipal Bond Funds

Thanks to the possibility of tax-exempt income from the state where municipal bonds are issued, there are a large number of different municipal bond funds in addition to the general funds. The general funds offer different maturities.

National Short-Term Municipal Bond Funds

National short-term municipal bond funds focus on maturities of less than five years, although it is important to understand if a fund tends toward the high end (five years) or low end (one year) of the range. This will give you an idea of the expected return. Most funds invest in investment-grade bonds and are diversified geographically, but don't assume this is always the case, as funds may concentrate investments in one state.

National Intermediate Municipal Bond Funds

Intermediate municipal bond funds fall in the 3- to 10-year maturity range. As you move up the maturity scale (and the risk/return scale) some funds will add a small percentage of less than investment grade bonds or foreign bonds to their portfolios. These may provide a return boost if yields on intermediate bonds are not sufficiently higher than short-term bonds to warrant the extra risk.

National Long-Term Municipal Bonds

Long-term municipal bond funds invest in bonds with maturities that exceed 10 years. They may also invest in bonds subject to the Alternative Minimum Tax, so be aware of that concern, which was discussed in Chapter 7. These funds seek high current income and should deliver for the risk you take with the interest rate exposure.

Single State Intermediate Municipal Bond Funds

A unique characteristic of municipal bonds is that they may be exempt from state taxes if the issue is bought by a resident of the state in which the bond was issued. This makes the income free from federal, state, and local taxes. Triple exemption of bond interest income is very appealing to people in high income tax brackets. The funds are offered for those states with high personal income tax rates. If you don't live in one of these states or are in a low federal income tax bracket, these funds are not for you. New York and California are popular states for offering these types of funds because of their high state income tax rates and relatively high per-capita incomes. The funds invest in bonds with maturities of less than 10 years.

Bond Tip

When considering single state bond mutual funds, be sure to apply the same analysis we used in Chapter 8 to look at tax equivalent yield. This will help you understand if this is a good buy for you.

Single State Long Municipal Bond Funds

These bond funds are similar to the intermediate with two exceptions. They stretch the maturities of their investments past 10 years and often a portion of their holdings are subject to the Alternative Minimum Tax.

Other Types of Bond Mutual Funds

There are a number of different bond mutual funds that are worth noting. These funds offer opportunities in low-cost investing and participating in more narrow markets, both domestic and abroad.

Bond Index Mutual Funds

There are many financial advisors who will tell you that index funds for both stocks and bonds are the only way to go. Index funds track a major indicator in the stock or bond market by replicating all or a substantial part of the holdings represented by the index. For example, in the stock market the S&P 500 stock index is a major market barometer.

Mutual funds that track the S&P 500 are among the most popular on the market.

One of the reasons is index fund investing is the ultimate buy-and-hold investment. There is no need to rebalance your portfolio or make adjustments—the fund automatically adjusts to any changes in the index. One of the main reasons the funds work is that the major providers (Vanguard invented index investing) can keep fund expenses very low. More of your investment dollars actually go into the fund to earn you money. This low-cost approach is popular and successful over the long term.

> **Bond Tip**
>
> Bond index funds represent the lowest-cost, most diversified buy you can make in bond funds. Their expenses are low and that helps them stay with the sector of the bond market they track.

Multi-Sector Bond Funds

Multi-sector bond funds seek the best return where they can find it. They are open to investing in bonds (both investment grade and below), pre-ferred stock, *REITs, convertible issues,* and a number of other securities. This freedom lets the fund manager pursue the best returns she can find. It also can make for some unsteady earnings if things don't go well.

def•i•ni•tion

> **Real Estate Investment Trusts (REITs)** are a special type of investment that sells a fixed number of shares. REITs invest in various types of real estate and pass 90 percent of the profits back to investors. REITs trade on stock markets like common stock.
>
> **Convertible issues** are bonds that allow the bondholder to convert the bond into shares of common stock under certain conditions and at a predetermined rate of exchange.

Convertible Bond Funds

Convertible bond funds invest a significant portion of their assets in convertible bonds and seek income and growth through appreciation. The funds may invest in foreign securities or below investment-grade bonds.

Ultrashort Bond Funds

These are money market funds for all practical purposes. They invest in short-term securities that reset their interest rates periodically or have maturities of less than one year.

International Bond Funds

International bond funds invest a significant portion of their assets in bonds or fixed income securities of foreign countries. Most will limit the percentage of the portfolio in any one country to no more than 25 percent. The fund manager often has great latitude so that he can move assets as economic and political conditions warrant. If there is a favorable relationship with the U.S. dollar, the fund can hold a significant percentage of assets in U.S. debt securities.

Emerging Markets Bond Funds

The emerging markets bond funds invest in debt and other securities issued by countries whose economies are beginning to grow from an agrarian past toward a more developed future. The fund manager may invest in investment- and below-investment-grade securities.

> **Bond Tip**
>
> Your best bet for investing in foreign bonds is probably through a good bond mutual fund. Investing in individual bonds is difficult enough, but when you layer in currency differences and political considerations, foreign bonds are hard to know.

Alternatives to Mutual Funds

You have several options to mutual funds when it comes to investing in bonds. Each of these alternatives offers some attractive features, but none combine the convenience and low cost of mutual funds.

Exchange-Traded Funds

Exchange-traded funds (ETFs) look like index mutual funds—they are baskets of stocks or bonds that track a particular index, either stocks or bonds. On the stock side, one of the most popular tracks the NASDAQ Composite. For bonds, the iShares Lehman Aggregate Bond is a good example.

An ETF is typically a fixed basket of securities that trades on the stock market like stocks do. It is priced with each trade and you can use trading strategies such as margin, selling short, and other market orders to profit from trading ETFs. You have to use a broker to trade ETFs, which means they are not suitable for investing small incremental amounts like mutual funds. Although you don't pay a fee to hold ETFs, you do pay a commission to both buy and sell them. If you have a large sum to invest, an ETF might make sense rather than a mutual fund. However, remember to factor in the commissions to buy and sell when figuring your return.

Closed-End Mutual Funds

Closed-end mutual funds are the less popular cousin of the more popular open-end mutual funds, although they are just known as mutual funds. The difference is that regular mutual funds continually take in new investors (and lose investors who redeem their shares), while a closed-end fund has a fixed number of shares and no more can be issued. Once all the shares of a closed-end fund are initially issued, they trade in the secondary market on the stock exchange.

Closed-end funds may borrow money to buy assets, which can increase their return or their losses, depending on how good their investment decisions are. You can find closed-end funds specializing in many of the same categories as regular mutual funds. Fund managers trade bonds in and out of the fund seeking the better yield.

Closed-end funds are sold through stockbrokers and some investment companies at issue and only through stockbrokers on the secondary market.

Market Place

Despite some attractive features, only ETFs have really captured the investing public's eye when you consider all the alternatives to open-end mutual funds.

Unit Investment Trusts

Unit investment trusts are like closed-end funds in that they are a fixed basket of securities that trades on the secondary market. Unlike the closed-end or open-end funds, the unit investment trust has a limited life. Once the bonds are acquired, there is no need for an investment manager because no assets are bought or sold. This keeps expenses extremely low, which is another attractive feature of unit trusts.

Bonds work well in unit investment trusts because bonds self-liquidate—they mature and repay the principal. A bond unit trust typically has a maturity date when the bulk of the bonds will mature. Up to that point, income from the bonds is passed to investors along with principal from bonds that mature before others. At some point, when there are only a small portion of the assets left in the trust, it liquidates the remaining bonds and distributes the proceeds to the investors.

Unit investment trusts do not trade in the secondary market. Sponsors may offer to buy back shares if you need to sell, but you will pay a sales fee. Unit trusts are most appropriate for investors with long holding periods. A front-end sales fee of several percent is not unusual and not onerous if you hold the unit trust for 7 to 10 years depending on the fee.

The Least You Need to Know

- Bond mutual funds have different benefits than investing in individual bonds.
- Bond mutual funds are managed by fund managers whose objectives may differ from yours.
- There are many different types of bond funds to fit almost any investing situation.
- There are alternatives to bond mutual funds, but none have the combination of benefits of bond mutual funds.

Planning a Bond Strategy

In This Chapter

- Financial expectations
- The perils of trading bonds
- Choosing a strategy
- Using some different bond products

Bonds should be a part of every investor's portfolio. The questions you must answer are what percentage is right for me and do I want to invest in individual bonds or bond mutual funds? As we delve into these topics in more depth other questions will present themselves, but these two major decisions frame how you will build your bond portfolio. The first question tends to be more about where you are in life and your tolerance for risk. The issue of investing in individual bonds or mutual funds may be more complicated for some of you. Investment strategies for each address the major concerns of most bond investors of income and preservation of capital. We'll wrap up the chapter and the book with a look at some different bond products that didn't get much coverage, specifically zero-coupon bonds and how you can use those as part of your investment strategies.

Setting Financial Goals

Everyone has a financial goal—they want to make more money. Unfortunately, that's not good enough when it comes to investing your money. You need to be very specific about where you want to go financially and what you expect of your investments. Bonds can be a big help because of their predictable income and return of principal.

Smoothing Out the Bumps

Bonds are not just for retired people. They can play an important role in everyone's portfolio by smoothing the rough peaks and valleys associated with the stock market. A mistake people make is looking just at how each individual investment has performed. While this is important, it is also important to step back and look at how your total package has done over a given period. This is where bonds can help if the stock market has had a rough period—bonds generally move in the opposite direction of stocks. If you have a reasonable presence of bonds in your portfolio, you will temper the harsh peaks and valleys of the stock market with the steady income bonds provide and the relative assurance of return of your principal.

Reaching Specific Goals Before Retirement

You can use bonds for much more than retirement planning. You can use them to target future financial needs by investing in a bond today that will pay a certain face value in the future. Zero-coupon bonds, which we look at in detail at the end of this chapter, are bought at a deep discount to face value and you redeem them for full face value at maturity. The difference is the interest earned. New parents could buy a 20-year zero-coupon bond for about $6,700 and redeem it for $20,000 to help pay for college. Your goal doesn't have to be that far off. You can use a series of bonds with different maturities but due on dates that you know you will need money for a down payment on a new house or a new car.

In these cases, you should use individual bonds to meet your specific goals because you will know exactly what the bonds will be worth on the dates they mature (assuming you invest in quality bonds). If you use a mutual fund for these purposes, you can't know what your shares will be worth on some future date. For the general purpose of accumulating assets in bonds, a bond mutual fund will work fine because you haven't set a specific dollar and date goal for the investment. It is easier and usually cheaper to accumulate assets in a bond mutual fund than it is to buy individual bonds.

Goals in Retirement

Most people look to bonds to meet certain financial goals in retirement: income to meet daily living expenses and capital preservation. For some retirees, tax-free income is important, which is available through investing in certain municipal bonds. Capital preservation is important because most retirees have no earned income to replace lost capital (as they might experience in the stock market). This is why most financial advisors urge retirees to have a significant portion of their assets in bonds and cash, while retaining a smaller amount in stocks to provide some protection against inflation.

Maximum Income or Stability and Return of Principal?

There is a case to be made that trading bonds for higher yields and capital gains is the way to earn maximum income from bond investing. Frankly, I don't buy it. Most investors are better off using bonds for their stability and return of principal.

Trading Bonds for Profit

There are investors who trade bonds in the secondary market for profit. They use trading techniques and strategies that let them earn profits on movement of market value. However, this is not a risk-free activity or an inexpensive one. Most investors don't have the time, experience, or knowledge of the bond market to make trading work on a regular basis. The high cost of transactions (markups, commissions, and so on) means you have to be right and there needs to be significant movement in the bond's market price for you to make a profit.

It can happen, but the odds are stacked against the individual investor.

Red Flag

Trading bonds is not for beginners and not for investors without a substantial amount of cash. Several hundred thousand dollars is necessary to get the best price on bonds and the lowest trading charges. That's a lot of money at risk.

Using Bonds for Bonds

Most investors are better off using bonds for their intended purpose: to provide a steady income and return of principal. These traits let you plan with confidence knowing that investment-grade bonds will usually meet their obligations (always if they are U.S. Treasury issues). Buying and holding intermediate maturing bonds is a good strategy for people at or near retirement, while others can choose bonds to fit a particular financial need or use a bond mutual fund to balance stock holdings.

Individual bonds have a beginning and an end (maturity). This allows you to plan for the income and return of principal. This is one of the main differences between bonds and bond funds. Bond funds are very useful for accumulating assets in bonds. The mutual funds allow you to invest modest amounts on a regular basis if that's what your budget allows and increase the amount as you are able.

If you buy new bonds at issue or directly from the U.S. Treasury, you can keep transaction costs to a minimum. Holding the bonds to maturity or call costs nothing and you get the semiannual income checks. When the bond matures, you receive the full face value of the bond and there are no extra costs to get your money back.

Bond Funds Have a Place, Too

Bond mutual funds don't behave the same way as individual bonds do. Because the fund manager's goal is growing share value, you may find income amounts are not as consistent as you would like. However, bond funds do offer some very significant advantages. For one, you can reinvest income back into the fund if you don't need it for living expenses. This grows your assets and saves you having to find another place to invest the money.

Bond funds also let you invest money in regular small (or big) increments. This investment strategy is not feasible with individual bonds. Bond funds make the most sense for people who need the balance bonds offer your portfolio, but don't necessarily need the income. Many people carry taxable bond funds in a retirement account, such as an IRA, to avoid current income tax on the income and capital gains.

The Bond Bottom Line

For many investors, it is not a question of using either a bond mutual fund or individual bonds, but the reality that both have a place in their portfolios. Individual bonds solve specific financial goals and can meet your long-term needs of income and capital preservation, while bond mutual funds are better vehicles for accumulating assets in bonds and buffering stock holdings.

> **Bond Tip**
>
> Bond funds and individual bonds are different tools for the same basic job. They aren't interchangeable, but you can build many of the same investment structures with either.

Investment Strategies

There is not one correct investment strategy and all others are wrong. What works for one investor may not work for you. Whether you use individual bonds, mutual funds, or a combination, is up to you. However, some guidelines are important to consider.

Bond Mutual Funds

Bond mutual funds fit many investor needs, such as diversification, convenience, liquidity, and others. However, you will pay for these benefits with expenses associated with the fund. Here are some considerations of bond mutual funds for your review.

- **Watch expenses**—Don't buy a mutual fund with a load or sales charge. Stick with no-load funds that have low expense ratios (Vanguard is a leader in low-cost funds).

- **Diversification**—Diversification is less important if you stick with high-quality (AAA-rated) bonds or U.S. Treasury issues. However, if you want to invest in high-yield corporate bonds (junk bonds), you definitely want the diversification a fund can give you.

- **Convenience**—Funds make it easy to invest with low minimums (many at $1,000) and most will automatically debit your checking account every month for a regular savings plan. If you deal directly with the investment company, you pay no transaction costs and no markup of the fund. You can get your money out quickly if you need it. Income from the fund can be reinvested to build your portfolio even quicker. You can hold a taxable bond mutual fund in your retirement account (IRA, for example) and defer taxes until you make withdrawals in retirement.

Market Place

With over 4,000 bond mutual funds, you can find one that will fit your needs. Using a service like www.MorningStar.com, you can find a fund that has the credit and investment goals that match yours.

Individual Bonds

Individual bonds have different attributes than a bond fund and can meet many personal financial goals. They have a beginning and an end and pay a steady income semiannually, which helps you with planning. Here are some considerations of individual bonds for your review:

- **New issues**—Only buy individual bonds at new issue to get the best pricing, since the issuer will pay sales fees. Buy U.S. Treasury issues directly from the Treasury.

- **Secondary market**—Avoid buying or selling bonds in the secondary market, if possible. Sales charges and obscured pricing make it difficult for you to profit in the environment, especially if you are a small investor. A "small" investor in the bond market is less than $500,000 to $1 million to invest.

- **Known value**—An individual bond will return a known value (its face value) at maturity plus pay interest income along the way. If you buy a highly rated bond, you can be reasonably sure the face value will be there at maturity. For example, if you buy a five-year bond with a face value of $10,000, you can be confident that in five years you'll have $10,000. With a bond fund, you don't know what your balance will be in five years.

- **No ongoing expenses**—If you buy your bond at issue and hold it until maturity, you have no ongoing cost of ownership.

With bond funds, even low-cost ones, there are operating expenses that come out of your investment assets each year.

- You control risk—With individual bonds, you control how much risk you want to take. Bond funds often have less well-defined limits on what risks they can take to achieve investment goals.

Asset Allocation

Asset allocation is the process of spreading your investment assets across different classes to increase the chances that if one class or type of investment has a bad run it will be offset in whole or in part by another class.

Asset Classes

There are three basic asset classes: stocks, bonds, and cash. How you allocate your assets among these classes is one of the most important investment decisions you'll make. Some research indicates this decision is more important than selecting the actual components of each class.

One of the investing variables you can control with asset allocation is volatility, or how much your portfolio fluctuates in value over a period. Stocks are notoriously volatile in the short term, yet provide the best historic returns in the long term. Bonds provide lower returns, but tend to be more stable.

No single asset allocation formula is correct for everyone. You must find your own that reflects where you are in life and how comfortable you are with volatility and risk. Most people in their younger years can afford to be more aggressive with their investing, which means more stocks and fewer bonds. On the other end of the scale, people at or approaching retirement need a more cautious approach that emphasizes preservation of capital, current income, and some protection against inflation. This normally indicates more bonds and fewer stocks.

Starting Point for Asset Allocation

One place to start with figuring your asset allocation mix is to subtract your age from 100. The result is how much you should invest in stocks. The remainder should be in bonds and cash instruments. For example, a 30-year-old investor would have 70 percent of her assets in stocks and 30 percent in bonds and cash. A 55-year-old investor would have 45 percent in stocks and 55 percent in bonds and cash.

This is simply a starting place. You may find it is too conservative for you or too volatile for a good night's sleep. Either decision is correct, because it's what's right for you. The important point is to understand the consequences of your decision.

A portfolio heavier in stocks is subject to the ups and downs the market is famous for, but also offers the best opportunity for superior returns (higher risk/higher potential rewards). More bonds means a steadier return and safety of principal if you invest in quality securities, but you will give up the possibility of exceptional returns (lower risk/steady, but lower returns).

> **Market Place**
>
> The market as defined as a broadly diversified portfolio of stocks has returned an average 11 percent over the past 70-plus years, while bonds have yielded around 7 percent.

What Building Blocks to Use

The choice between individual bonds and bond funds is, in part, a matter of personal taste. Both will help you meet your goals as we have noted. However, a few special bonds have not been fully covered yet that you may want to consider. Unlike the regular bonds we have discussed up to this point, these sophisticated securities may require the assistance of a professional financial advisor. Another strategy also discussed in detail in the last section of the chapter is called "laddering" bonds to protect against interest rate hikes.

Investing in Bonds for the Future

If you are investing in bonds for your retirement (as opposed to a specific goal like funding a college education), you can choose a number of routes.

Bond mutual funds make great vehicles for accumulating assets over a long period using dollar cost averaging. This technique is a good way to add to funds in a manner that is easy and can be put on automatic pilot by having the fund company debit your checking account for a fixed amount each week. (If you belong to a 401[k] or 403[b] retirement plan, you already are practicing dollar cost averaging: your monthly contribution to the plan.)

You can also use individual bonds, especially if you plan to buy and hold them to maturity. Zero-coupon bonds (see more below) are a good choice if you have a lump sum to invest and don't need current income for the life of the bond. If retirement is still years away, you can invest in highly rated long-term bonds and take advantage of yield premiums they offer—however, only if you plan to hold the bonds to maturity.

Zero-Coupon Bonds

Zero-coupon bonds are a different way of investing in bonds. Unlike regular bonds, zeros make no regular income payments, but are sold at a deep discount. The bonds are redeemed at full face value. The difference between the purchase price and face value is your earned interest. The longer the maturity, the deeper the discount off face value you purchase the bond. Zeros come in a variety of maturities. You can match a known need in the future with the face value of a zero-coupon bond.

The U.S. Treasury, corporations, and municipalities issue zero-coupon bonds. Treasury zeros are handled by private brokers and banks—you can't buy them directly from the Treasury like other issues.

Zero-coupon bonds don't pay interest, but that doesn't mean you don't pay taxes. One of the downsides of investing in zeros is that you are liable for taxes on the interest the bond accrues each year, even though you don't receive it. This means you have a tax bill from the bond every year, but no income. It also means you are paying taxes as you go, so you won't be hit with a huge tax bill when the bond matures.

> **Bond Tip**
>
> Zero-coupon bonds are very credit- and interest-rate sensitive. If the bond is downgraded or interest rates rise, the market value of zero-coupon bonds will drop significantly. You will still receive the face value at maturity, but if you need your money early, you may face a loss when you sell.

Asset Backed Securities

Asset Backed Securities (ABS) are a type of bond backed by financial assets other than mortgages. These securities are backed by receivables from credit cards, consumer finance companies, and companies that finance automobiles and manu-factured housing. These notes are variable in maturities just like most other securities, but most of them carry a very high rating (AAA) from the credit rating agencies.

This enhanced credit rating means the securities earn exceptional returns that are comparable to similarly rated corporate bonds, without the added risk. ABS bonds can be complicated because they are tied to pools of loans. Some of those loans amortize—that is, pay principal and interest—such as auto loans, while others might just pay mainly interest, such as credit card–backed ABS bonds. Your financial professional can help you find the right ABS for your situation. Unless you buy a mutual fund that invests in ABS bonds, this is not a security for beginning investors.

Collateralized Mortgage Obligations

Collateralized Mortgage Obligations (CMOs) are bonds backed by mortgages, very much like ABS bonds. However, CMOs offer some very sophisticated qualities that set them apart from other bonds. Investment bankers and other financial institutions strip the income streams off these bonds and repackage them to investors needing immediate income.

These sophisticated securities revolve around mortgages and the pass-through securities associated with financing mortgage loans in today's market. Pass-through securities allow institutions to strip the cash off a note and resell that income stream to another investor. The principal of the note remains intact and is sold as another form of collateral. The income streams are directed to investors looking for immediate income and they are allowed to choose when they want to receive their income. Different classes of investors receive interest and principal payments on a schedule that meets their financial needs. Again, these are complicated products and your financial professional can help you understand if CMOs are right for you.

International or World Bonds

You can buy bonds from a number of different countries, often at very favorable yields. All the risks of domestic bonds apply to foreign bonds, plus some additional considerations. Anytime you invest outside the United States, you should be worried about whether your investment is denominated in dollars or the local currency. If it is in the local currency, you should be aware of exchange rates and how they fluctuate on a daily basis. For most investors, a practical solution to investing in foreign bonds is to do so through a mutual fund. You may find these carry a higher than normal expense load, but some of these funds have done quite well in emerging markets.

> **Red Flag**
>
> The bond market is no different from any other market where there is a lot of money at stake—scam artists and crooks will find a way to part you from your money if you aren't careful. Don't respond to unsolicited e-mails or phone calls. If it appears too good to be true—guess what?

Building a Bond Ladder to Success

As we've seen, interest rate changes can be disastrous for bondholders. If rates go up, you are stuck with bonds that pay a lower rate than new bonds offer. If rates go down, you may earn a premium for a period, but when your bond matures, you will have to reinvest the proceeds in a bond that pays a lower rate than you received from your old bond.

It is not a good idea to try to guess where interest rates are going to be in three years or five years. There is another way to protect yourself against rate hikes and earn the highest possible rate at the same time. It is called laddering; it works on bonds and, incidentally, bank certificates of deposit. Here's how it works.

Say you have $50,000 to invest. Rather than put it into one or two bonds, you could consider building a bond ladder. You do this by buying 10 bonds of $5,000 each. One matures in one year, the next in two years, the next in three years, and so on. You now own 10 bonds with maturities ranging from one year to ten years. When the one-year bond matures, you now have nine bonds with the oldest maturity of nine years. You use the proceeds from the maturing one-year bond and buy a new ten-year bond.

This cycle of replacing the longest bond with proceeds from the shortest bond means you will get the best rate each year (assuming a traditional yield curve where long rates are higher than short rates). You also have a bond maturing each year, which gives you the capital to invest in a new long bond.

It's not a foolproof system. If interest rates are skewed so that long rates are lower than short rates, you will be giving up higher rates by buying a long bond each year. There is nothing particularly magic about using ten years. I don't believe your ladder needs to be any longer than that and it could certainly be shorter; however, I wouldn't do less than five years.

The Least You Need to Know

- Financial goals for your investment in bonds should be specific and targeted to your needs at different times in your life.

- Both individual bonds and bond mutual funds have benefits and drawbacks when it comes to meeting specific goals.

- Bonds and bond funds have a role in your investment strategy, which starts with determining your asset allocation.

- Bond investors have many choices in building a portfolio; some securities are easy to understand, while others may require the advice of a financial professional.

Appendix A

Glossary

accrued interest Accrued interest is interest earned, but not yet paid.

ask price The price the seller wants for a bond.

asset class An asset class is a group of similar assets that share risk and reward features. Broad asset classes are stocks, bonds, and cash. There are much more refined classes within each of those.

basis point A basis point equals one one-hundredth of one percent (0.01 percent). There are 100 basis points in one percentage point. Bond yields are quoted in basis points.

bid The price a buyer will pay for a bond.

bond swap Selling one bond and purchasing another of similar market value. It is usually done to record a tax loss, but it can also be used to replace a bond with one that has a different maturity or credit quality.

call provision A call provision describes the dates when the issuer can call or redeem the bond, which will be before the natural maturity of the bond. Issuers call old bonds to replace them with new bonds when interest rates have dropped.

capital intensive Some businesses require much more capital to operate than others. Businesses such as transportation (airlines, railroads, and so on) need lots of money to operate. That is why they are said to be capital intensive.

CMO (Collateralized Mortgage Obligation) Collateralized Mortgage Obligations are bonds that separate mortgages into different classes to meet different maturity needs.

Consumer Price Index (CPI) The CPI is the primary measurement of inflation. It measures a basket of goods and services considered vital to everyday life and marks the increase or decline in these goods over time. The Bureau of Labor Statistics issues the CPI and other inflation measurements monthly.

coupon Coupon represents the interest payment due on a bond. A $1,000 bond with a 6% coupon will pay $60 in interest annually.

current yield The current yield is the interest paid as a percentage of the current market price.

CUSIP (Committee on Uniform Security Identification Procedures) This committee developed a system of coding securities with a unique nine-digit number for tracking purposes. All modern securities have a CUSIP number.

debenture A debenture is an unsecured bond—an IOU backed by the issuer's promise to pay.

discount   A bond with a coupon interest rate lower than market interest rates will have a market value lower than par and is said to be trading at a discount to par.

dollar cost averaging   Dollar cost averaging is an investment strategy that says you should invest the same amount on a regular basis to achieve the best average price. For example, if you invest $25 every two weeks in a bond mutual fund, you can buy shares at the current price. If share prices are up, you buy fewer shares and if share prices are down, you buy more shares. Over time, your average share price is lower than if you tried to time the market with buys.

duration   Duration is the percentage change in a bond's price given a percentage change in the yield on the bond. The higher the duration, the more sensitive the bond is to interest rate changes.

Exchange-traded fund   Exchange-traded funds are very much like mutual funds, but they trade like stocks on the open market. They represent bundles of stocks or bonds and are bought through a stockbroker.

face value   Face value (also called face amount) is the same as par value and principal. It is the amount shown on the face of the bond.

general obligation bond   General obligation bonds are issued by municipalities and backed by their ability to collect taxes and other revenues.

high-yield bond High-yield bonds, also known as junk bonds, are issued by corporations with low credit ratings. They offer a high yield, but are risky.

indenture agreement The indenture agreement is a binding legal document between the organization issuing the bonds and the bondholder. It details the maturity, interest payments, collateral, and other important information.

issuer An issuer is the entity (U.S. Treasury, agency, municipality, or corporation) that issues the bonds.

junk bond Junk bonds, also known as high-yield bonds, are issued by corporations with low credit ratings. They offer a high yield, but are risky.

market value The market value of a bond is what it will bring in the secondary market. This value may be more or less than the face value depending on whether market interest rates are higher or lower than the coupon interest rate. A change in the credit rating could also affect the market value.

markup The markup on a bond's price is the difference paid by the purchaser between the retail price and wholesale price, which is the price in the interdealer market. Markdown would be the difference received at the retail level on the price of a bond off the wholesale price.

maturity A bond's maturity is the date when the bond owner is due the full face value of the bond.

municipality   In the world of municipal bonds, municipality refers to any state, county, township, city, and so on that issues bonds. It could also be a tax district such as a utility, road, or sewer. Municipal bonds include securities issued by all sorts of government entities and agencies at the state or lower level.

par value   Par value is the same as face amount and principal. A bond is said to be selling at par when it sells for the face amount.

premium   A bond whose coupon interest rate is higher than market interest rates will have a market value above par and is said to be trading at a premium to par.

principal   Principal is the face amount of the bond or the amount paid at maturity.

revenue bond   A revenue bond is issued by a municipality and is backed by tolls, rents, or fees paid by users of the projects constructed with the bonds.

secondary market   The secondary market is the open market between individuals or through an exchange where previously issued bonds are bought and sold. A bond can be bought and sold many times before its maturity.

syndicate   A syndicate is formed by a group of investment banking firms to underwrite a bond issue too large for one firm to manage on its own.

transparency Transparency refers to how easy or hard it is to find information, especially pricing, on securities. Bond pricing often lacks transparency, and that puts individual investors at a disadvantage.

underwriter An investment banking firm underwrites or guarantees the sale of the bond issue, often buying the whole issue outright if possible. The investment bank then sells the bonds to large institutional buyers and, in some cases, part of the issue may go to retail brokers for sale to the public.

yield Yield is the rate of return earned by a bond. It is expressed as a percentage and is a function of the bond's purchase price and coupon interest rate.

yield curve The yield curve is the plotting of short-, intermediate-, and long-term interest rates to observe the relationship. U.S. Treasury issues are often used since they have no credit risk to distort the interest rates.

yield to maturity Yield to maturity is a complicated calculation that assumes a bond is held to maturity and coupon payments are reinvested to earn interest, along with any capital gain or loss at maturity. Most people use an online calculator or sophisticated software to make the calculation.

Further Resources

Compared to the resources available to stock investors, bond investors have much less to draw on for help. Most (93 percent) of all bonds are owned by institutional investors. Many individual investors choose to add bonds to their portfolios through mutual funds or exchange-traded funds—both are workable options. If you want to buy individual bonds, especially corporate or municipal bonds, you may find it difficult to locate good information to help you make informed decisions.

Here are some of the best resources for news and information about bonds and the economy. The list is not as long as it would be for investors interested in information on stocks, but these are good resources.

Newspapers, Magazines, and Reports

Most financial newspapers and magazines devote the majority of their coverage to stocks and personal finance issues. Here are some publications that give bonds more coverage than the average publication.

The Wall Street Journal. The Journal, as it is often called, is one of the few newspapers to regularly report bond prices and information for bond investors. In addition, if you want to stay on top of economic news, it's the undisputed authority. The paper is also online at www.wsj.com for a subscription.

Barron's. For top-notch market and economic coverage, Barron's is one of the best financial publications out there. Bond coverage is not as specific as the markets in general and the economy, but a great place for insight. It has an online subscription site at www.barrons.com.

Forbes. Forbes has been publishing business and investing news for many years, and there is a reason it is still popular. The magazine and accompanying website—www.forbes.com—are a good source of business and market news. The website features a section on bonds, although like most sites not dedicated to bonds, it is not very deep.

Standard & Poor's CreditWeek. This report details information on domestic and foreign credit markets. You can also find scheduled and recent bond issues, both corporate and municipal. Standard & Poor's Bond Guide and Standard & Poor's Corporation Records are complementary products that cover bonds and issuers in detail. This is a very expensive service, so look for a copy at a large library or at your broker's office.

Moody's Credit Perspectives. This is also a very expensive report covering credit markets and news. It includes analysis and credit ratings of bond issues. Your library or broker are your best places to look for this report. More information at Moodys.com.

Mergent Bond Record. This monthly report covers 68,000 bond and related credit issues. It is offered by subscription along with *Mergent's Annual Bond Record,* which is a comprehensive look at corporate and municipal issues. You can find more information at www.mergent.com.

Online Resources

Websites devoted exclusively to bonds number many fewer than those focused on stocks and personal finance. Most of the good business and market information sites have an area that covers bonds; however, it usually occupies only a small portion of the whole site. There are many good websites with information on companies for researching corporate bonds. You can also find information on bond mutual funds online.

Websites for Information on Bonds

U.S. Savings Bonds Online (www.savingbonds.gov). This is the U.S. Treasury site for its debt products including bills, notes, bonds, and the other products covered in Chapter 5, but not agency bonds. This is one of the most informative and helpful investing sites you'll visit. You can learn about the products and sign up for an account to buy directly from the Treasury.

Investing in Bonds.com (www.investinginbonds. com). This is one of the best websites for information on bonds that doesn't try to sell you something. The site is run by the Bond Market Association, so I guess you could say they are selling the concept of bond investing. The site has an abundance of information on all types of bonds and includes some price data. For information on corporate and municipal bonds, this is your first stop.

BondsOnline.com (www.bondsonline.com). The site offers news and commentary on bonds as well as educational material. A lengthy listing of bonds for sale is helpful for those looking to buy at issue.

BONDTALK.com (www.bondtalk.com). An informative site with news and analysis for bond investors. It has a good education section and glossary.

Bloomberg.com (www.bloomberg.com). Bloomberg is one of the premier information sources on investing and business. Most of its offerings are sold through subscription to stockbrokers, institutional investors, and so on. The site does have a free bond section that offers prices and information such as calls issued for municipal bond issues.

SmartMoney.com (www.smartmoney.com). This is a good all-round site with a strong bond section that has prices, economic information, calendars, and educational material.

YahooFinance.com (www.YahooFinance.com). YahooFinance has a strong section on bonds including a list of upcoming issues. Investors looking to buy new issues can get a look at what's coming up.

Information About Corporations

Reuters.com (www.Reuters.com). Reuters has one of the best financial profile services (for free) on the Internet. If you want to know more about a company's financial health, this is an excellent place to start. If you are not familiar with all the ratios and indicators the site uses, it offers explanations to help you understand the numbers.

CNNMoney.com (www.CNNMoney.com). Like its all-news mother site, CNNMoney is on top of market and economic news and reports it in a very accessible manner. It covers bonds along with the rest of the market; however, it shines in reporting business news stories.

EDGAR (www.sec.gov/edgar). EDGAR is the SEC's database of the reports and forms public companies must file. You can find annual reports and much more here. EDGAR is free, but not easy to use. There are services that will do your research for you for a fee.

MSN Money.com (www.moneycentral.msn.com). MSN Money is another top-notch information and education site. It is part of the Microsoft world and devotes considerable resources to the collection of information.

Briefing.com (www.Briefing.com). One important feature of this website is the calendar, which shows upcoming financial events—some of which may move the market. Many of these events are economic announcements which can affect bond prices and they can get confusing if you don't stay current.

Information on Bond Mutual Funds and Exchange-Traded Funds

MorningStar.com (www.morningstar.com). MorningStar.com is hands-down the premier site for researching mutual funds. The site has an extensive section on bond funds, exchange-traded funds, and educational material. The basic site is free; however, for a modest monthly subscription you can access their premium content. This service includes recommendations and more in-depth looks at products.

Marketwatch.com (www.Marketwatch.com). Experts analyze bond funds and their managers while not charging you a single penny. This is one of the best sites for commentary.

Investment Company Institute (www.ici.org). This is a trade association-sponsored website for mutual funds with a section on bond funds. It is educational and presents the material in a manner that is accessible.

Index

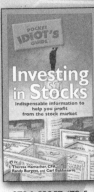